Charity Giving Donation Revelation

Your Great Big Grab Bag of Useless Helpful Tidbits

Michael Clutton

Published by Michael Clutton, 2024.

While every precaution has been taken in the preparation of this book, the publisher assumes no responsibility for errors or omissions, or for damages resulting from the use of the information contained herein.

CHARITY GIVING DONATION REVELATION

First edition. June 14, 2024.

ISBN: 979-8227648471

Written by Michael Clutton.

Table of Contents

The Joys and Pitfalls of Charitable Giving

Welcome to the zany, heartwarming, and occasionally perplexing world of charitable giving! Whether you're a seasoned philanthropist or just looking to give back a little, this book is your ultimate guide. Use it to navigating the often-murky waters of donations with a smile on your face and a dollar in your hand.

Charitable giving, at its core, is a beautiful thing. Contribute to a better world, one small step at a time. However, let's be honest: charity has its own quirks and challenges. Have you ever wondered why there's always that one guy dressed as a giant banana on the corner, shaking a tin can? Or why some charities spend more on fancy galas than on actual causes? Well, you're not alone!

In these pages, we'll plunge into the joys and absurdities of charitable giving, offering you plenty of laughs along the way. From heartwarming success stories to eyebrow-raising scams, we'll cover it all. During our journey, we'll equip you with the knowledge to make wise choices with your hard-earned money.

Now, before we get too far, let's address the elephant in the room: religious donations. We've opted not to cover donations to religious organizations in detail here. However, it's worth noting that this area can be particularly tricky.

TV evangelists, anyone?

Some religious leaders have used faith to make money, and some pseudo-religions have amassed wealth with no charitable intentions. While religious giving is important, it's crucial to be cautious when donating to religious entities. Always do your homework to ensure your generosity supports genuine causes.

So, buckle up and get ready for a wild ride through the world of charitable giving. Whether you're looking to donate a little or a lot, we've got you covered with practical tips, amusing anecdotes, and a healthy dose of skepticism. Let's make the world a better place—together, and with a grin!

Chapter 1: The History of Charitable Giving

Overview of Early Charities

Charitable giving has deep roots across various cultures and time periods. In ancient Egypt, tomb inscriptions linked spirituality and charity by seeking blessings for those who gave to the needy. In ancient Greece, they had a practice called liturgies. Wealthy citizens would fund public projects and celebrations to encourage community responsibility. Imagine the ancient Greek version of Kickstarter: "Donate 50 drachmas and get a front-row seat at the symposium!"

In ancient Rome, the government supported banquets, games, and helped the poor by giving them discounted grain. Think of it as the original food stamps program, but with more togas and fewer bureaucratic hurdles.

In medieval Europe, the Church was the primary driver of charity. Monasteries and convents provided food, shelter, and medical care to those in need as part of their religious duty to give to the less fortunate. If you were down on your luck, you could count on a monk to provide a meal and a bed—no Yelp reviews necessary. Religious organizations like the Knights Hospitaller and the Order of St. Lazarus cared for the sick and destitute.

Evolution Over Centuries

The Renaissance and Enlightenment periods marked significant shifts in charitable giving. Wealthy individuals began establishing endowments and trusts to fund hospitals, schools, and other public services. It was like the original "Go Fund Me" but with fancier wigs and ruffled collars. During this time, many ancient charities were established, such as London's Christ's Hospital in 1552. This organization focused on educating children who had lost their parents. It turns out that even back then, people knew that kids without parents could use a little extra help—preferably with fewer plagues involved.

In the 19th century, philanthropy became more organized, thanks to people like Andrew Carnegie and John D. Rockefeller. They created foundations to help solve social problems. Like the original "Sharks," they were philanthropists who invested in important things such as libraries and public health. "Scientific philanthropy" emerged, which focuses on using data and research to make charitable efforts more effective. Because who wouldn't want to add a little science to their generosity? It's like upgrading from a wooden abacus to a shiny new calculator.

Modern Charitable Landscape

In the 21st century, charitable giving has transformed dramatically. Charities can now use social media and online platforms to reach more people globally and raise resources more efficiently. Save the world with just one click, even in your pajamas. Websites like GoFundMe and Kickstarter have made it easier for people to support causes they care about through crowdfunding. It's like throwing a virtual bake sale where everyone's invited, but no one has to worry about burning the cookies.

Contemporary charities address a range of issues, from local community needs to global challenges. Groups like Doctors Without Borders and the Bill and Melinda Gates Foundation use smart plans and information to tackle health issues and poverty. They're the superheroes of philanthropy, armed with spreadsheets and medical kits instead of capes and laser vision. Local grassroots movements also play a critical role, addressing specific needs within communities. Think of them as the neighborhood superheroes, swooping in to save the day with a potluck dinner and a lot of heart.

Useless Helpful Tidbits

- **Oldest Recorded Charity**: The King's School, Canterbury, founded in 597 AD by St. Augustine, originally established to educate poor boys, still operates today as a prestigious school.
- **Surprising Sources of Donations**: In 2013, Allen Swift of Massachusetts left $4 million to a local hospital, having lived frugally and kept his 1928 Rolls-Royce in working condition for 82 years.
- **Different Cultural Approaches to Charity**: In Japan, the concept of *tsunagu* emphasizes connecting people through acts of kindness, with companies often donating a portion of their profits regularly. In Islamic cultures, *zakat*—one of the Five Pillars of Islam—requires Muslims to give a fixed percentage of their savings to those in need.
- **First Crowdfunding Campaign:** The Statue of Liberty's pedestal was funded by one of the first recorded crowdfunding efforts in 1885. Over 160,000 donors contributed more than $100,000 (equivalent

to about $2.5 million today), proving that even back then, people were willing to chip in for a good cause—especially if it involved a giant statue.

- **Early Modern Philanthropy:** In the 18th century, Thomas Coram established the Foundling Hospital in London, the UK's first dedicated charity for abandoned children. Coram spent 17 years campaigning to secure funding and royal endorsement, showcasing early modern determination in philanthropy.

Charitable giving is diverse, with each culture having its own unique practices and philosophies in helping others. People's desire to improve the world has been constant throughout history.

Chapter 2: Nonprofits and Popular Charities

Definition and Structure of Nonprofits

Nonprofit organizations, also known as NGOs or charities, work for the public good instead of making money. Think of them as the do-gooders of the world, turning dollars into deeds. These organizations use surplus funds to support education, healthcare, social services, and the environment. Basically, they're like Robin Hood, but with more paperwork and fewer arrows. Nonprofits don't have to pay federal income taxes on donations, so they can use more funds for their charitable activities. It's like getting a free pass from Uncle Sam to save the world.

Nonprofits rely on directors to oversee operations. At the same time, a team of dedicated staff and volunteers work hard to carry out the organization's programs, fueled by coffee and goodwill. To effectively use donor funds for the organization's mission, it is important to be transparent and accountable. After all, nothing keeps a charity on its toes like the thought of an army of donors armed with magnifying glasses and a lot of questions.

Profiles of Popular Charities

1. Red Cross

The Red Cross is synonymous with emergency response and humanitarian aid. Founded in 1863, it operates in nearly every country, providing disaster relief, blood donations, and emergency assistance. However, it's not without its controversies. After Hurricane Sandy, the Red Cross received criticism for how it used funds. Reports suggested that a large amount went towards administrative costs instead of direct aid.

- **Financial Efficiency**: According to Charity Navigator, the American Red Cross spends about 89% of its budget on programs and services. Critics say the organization should be more open about how it spends donations during major disasters.

2. American Cancer Society (ACS)

Founded in 1913, the ACS is dedicated to eliminating cancer through research, education, advocacy, and patient services. The organization has done a lot for cancer research and awareness, but people have questioned how they handle money.

- **Financial Efficiency**: Approximately 75% of the ACS's budget goes toward its programs and services. Concerns have been raised about the remaining 25% being used for fundraising and administrative expenses. For instance, in 2019, the ACS spent over $140 million on fundraising alone.

3. American Heart Association (AHA)

Since 1924, the AHA has been a leading force in the fight against heart disease and stroke. It raises money for heart research, teaches people about healthy living, and lobbies for improved public health policies.

- **Financial Efficiency**: The AHA allocates about 79% of its budget to research, public health education, and community services. However, some donors and watchdog groups want more transparency in how funds are distributed, especially regarding executive salaries and administrative costs.

4. Médecins Sans Frontières (Doctors Without Borders)

Founded in 1971, Médecins Sans Frontières (MSF) provides medical care in conflict zones and areas affected by disease outbreaks. MSF is renowned for its rapid response and commitment to impartial and independent humanitarian action.

- **Financial Efficiency**: MSF spends around 85% of its budget on program activities. It has been praised for its transparency and effective use of funds.

5. UNICEF

The United Nations Children's Fund (UNICEF) works in over 190 countries and territories to save children's lives, defend their rights, and help them fulfill their potential. UNICEF's work includes vaccination, education, emergency relief, and more.

- **Financial Efficiency**: UNICEF spends about 88% of its budget on programs for children. It is well-regarded for its extensive reach and impact.

6. Habitat for Humanity

Founded in 1976, Habitat for Humanity builds and renovates affordable housing for families in need. The organization works globally to tackle housing issues and promote sustainable development.

- **Financial Efficiency**: Habitat for Humanity allocates about 77% of its budget to program services. Its volunteer-driven model helps maximize the impact of donations.

7. The Nature Conservancy

Since 1951, The Nature Conservancy has worked to conserve the lands and waters on which all life depends. Their efforts involve gaining land, promoting sustainability, and establishing conservation easements.

- **Financial Efficiency**: The Nature Conservancy spends approximately 76% of its budget on conservation programs. It is praised for its science-based approach to environmental protection.

8. World Wildlife Fund (WWF)

Founded in 1961, the WWF focuses on wilderness preservation and the reduction of human impact on the environment. The organization works on protecting wildlife, addressing climate change, and promoting sustainable development.

- **Financial Efficiency**: The WWF allocates about 79% of its budget to conservation activities. It is known for its global campaigns and partnerships.

9. St. Jude Children's Research Hospital

Founded in 1962 by entertainer Danny Thomas, St. Jude leads research and treatment of pediatric catastrophic diseases. Families never receive a bill for treatment, travel, housing, or food.

- **Financial Efficiency**: St. Jude spends approximately 82% of its budget on research and patient care. It is highly regarded for its commitment to treating and curing childhood diseases.

10. Feeding America

Feeding America is the nation's largest domestic hunger-relief organization. It works through a network of food banks to distribute food to those in need.

- **Financial Efficiency**: Feeding America spends about 98% of its budget on programs. It is praised for its efficiency and impact in addressing food insecurity.

11. Save the Children

Founded in 1919, Save the Children focuses on improving the lives of children worldwide through education, health care, and emergency relief. They are known for their rapid response to disasters and long-term programs aimed at sustainable development.

- Financial Efficiency: Approximately 85% of their budget goes toward programs and services. They are praised for their effective use of funds and comprehensive annual reports.

12. World Vision

World Vision is a Christian organization that helps children and families in almost 100 countries since 1950. Their work includes emergency relief, education, health care, and economic development.

- Financial Efficiency: About 87% of their budget is allocated to programs. Despite facing criticism for their religious beliefs, they are valued for their impactful work.

13. Oxfam

Established in 1942, Oxfam is a global organization that fights inequality to end poverty and injustice. They prioritize a fair economy, gender equality, climate change action, and community recovery and growth.

- Financial Efficiency: Oxfam spends around 78% of its budget on programs. The organization has had some internal problems but still plays a crucial role in fighting global poverty.

14. CARE

Founded in 1945, CARE delivers emergency relief and long-term international development projects. Their work includes fighting global poverty, improving health, and advancing gender equality.

- Financial Efficiency: CARE allocates about 90% of its budget to programs. The organization is known for its efficiency and transparency in reporting.

15. International Rescue Committee (IRC)

The IRC was founded in 1933 at the request of Albert Einstein to help those suffering under Nazi oppression. Today, it responds to the world's worst humanitarian crises and helps people survive, recover, and rebuild their lives.

- Financial Efficiency: Approximately 87% of their budget is spent on programs. The IRC is highly regarded for its impactful work in conflict zones and disaster-stricken areas.

16. Plan International

Founded in 1937, Plan International advances children's rights and equality for girls. They work in over 75 countries, focusing on education, health, and community development.

- Financial Efficiency: Plan International dedicates around 82% of its budget to programs. They are recognized for their strong advocacy and effective community-based projects.

17. Amnesty International

Founded in 1961, Amnesty International is a global movement of more than 10 million people who campaign to end abuses of human rights. They investigate and expose human rights abuses, and mobilize public pressure to bring abusers to justice.

- Financial Efficiency: Around 80% of their budget goes to programs. Amnesty International is well-known for its rigorous research and impactful advocacy work.

18. The Salvation Army

The Salvation Army, founded in 1865, offers various social services like disaster relief, rehabilitation, and aid for the homeless. They operate in over 130 countries.

- Financial Efficiency: The Salvation Army spends about 82% of its budget on programs. Even though people worry about their religious beliefs, they are still inclusive when it comes to social services.

19. Goodwill Industries

Goodwill, established in 1902, supports people with disabilities or disadvantages; providing job training, employment help, and community programs. Their thrift stores fund these initiatives.

- Financial Efficiency: Approximately 84% of their budget supports job training and community programs. Goodwill is noted for its sustainable business model that supports local communities.

20. Heifer International

Heifer International has been helping communities for 75 years; giving them animals and agricultural training, so they can become self-sufficient. Their model promotes sustainable agriculture and economic development.

- Financial Efficiency: Heifer International allocates about 76% of its budget to programs. They are well-regarded for their innovative approach to poverty alleviation and community empowerment.

Success Stories and Impact
Red Cross

The Red Cross helped during the pandemic by giving blood, responding to disasters, and supporting communities to save lives. The organization helped with vaccinations, gave out protective gear, and set up quarantine shelters. It was challenging for them to offer resources and mental health support to frontline workers and affected communities.

American Cancer Society (ACS)

The ACS's funding has been crucial for cancer research, leading to enormous improvements in cancer survival rates. Their Relay for Life events have raised millions for research and patient support. Some think the organization should prioritize research and patient care over fundraising and administration.

American Heart Association (AHA)

The AHA's Go Red for Women campaign has raised awareness about heart disease in women, improving prevention and treatment. Their efforts have significantly contributed to public health education and cardiovascular research. People often wonder how funds are divided, especially when it comes to executive salaries and administrative expenses.

Médecins Sans Frontières (Doctors Without Borders)

MSF's rapid response to the Ebola outbreak in West Africa saved thousands of lives and helped contain the epidemic. Their work during the COVID-19 pandemic showed their ability to provide crucial care in emergencies. MSF is known for being transparent and using funds effectively, with much of their budget going towards program activities.

UNICEF

UNICEF's vaccination programs have significantly reduced child mortality rates worldwide. Their extensive reach and impact on emergency relief and long-term development have been well-regarded. Yet, finding a balance between immediate relief and sustainable development remains a complex challenge.

Habitat for Humanity

Through their global village program, Habitat for Humanity has built and improved housing for over 29 million people. Their volunteer-driven model maximizes the impact of donations. Yet, the organization faces issues with logistics and receives criticism about project sustainability.

The Nature Conservancy

The Nature Conservancy saved lots of land in the Amazon rainforest, keeping important ecosystems safe. People like how they use science to protect the environment but worry about their partnerships with big companies.

World Wildlife Fund (WWF)

WWF's efforts in saving the giant panda from extinction have been globally recognized as a conservation success story. Their global campaigns and partnerships have had significant impacts on wildlife conservation. WWF has accomplished a lot. But they still face difficulties in carrying out projects and working with controversial industries.

St. Jude Children's Research Hospital

Thanks to St. Jude's research, more kids with cancer are surviving than ever before. Their model of not charging families for treatment ensures comprehensive support. However, it's difficult to maintain this level of care without enough funding.

Feeding America

Feeding America's network of 200 food banks and 60,000 food pantries serves millions of people each year. Their programs and partnerships have successfully reduced hunger in the U.S., but they now need to address the growing demand for food assistance.

Useless Helpful Tidbits

- **Statistics on the Most Popular Charities Globally**: According to Charity Navigator, the American Red Cross, UNICEF, and Médecins Sans Frontières consistently rank among the most popular charities worldwide.

- **Notable Achievements of Famous Nonprofits**: Médecins Sans Frontières won the Nobel Peace Prize in 1999 for their medical work in conflict zones. UNICEF has played a pivotal role in nearly eradicating polio through widespread vaccination campaigns.

- **Quirky Facts About Famous Nonprofits**: The Salvation Army's red kettles, seen during the holiday season, began in 1891 when a Salvation Army captain wanted to raise funds to feed San Francisco's poor. The idea caught on and now the kettles are a holiday staple.

- **Need for Caution**: While popular charities like the American Cancer Society, Red Cross, and Heart Association do significant work, donors should know how funds are allocated. For example, in 2019, the American Cancer Society spent over $140 million on fundraising alone. Before donating, check financial reports and ratings from organizations like Charity Navigator and GuideStar. Make sure your money is being used effectively.

Chapter 3: The Most Productive Charities

Criteria for Productivity

To figure out how productive a charity is, we look at different factors that show how well they use their resources to accomplish their mission. The most critical criteria include:

- **Financial Efficiency**: The percentage of donations that directly support the charity's programs versus administrative and fundraising costs.
- **Transparency and Accountability**: Clear reporting of financial statements, program outcomes, and operational practices.
- **Impact and Outcomes**: Tangible results and measurable improvements in the issues the charity aims to address.
- **Sustainability**: Long-term viability and the ability to continue making a difference over time.
- **Donor Engagement**: Effective communication with donors and maintaining trust through consistent updates and transparency.

Top Productive Charities

1. Wounded Warrior Project (WWP) The Wounded Warrior Project supports injured veterans through a variety of programs aimed at improving their physical and mental health, aiding their recovery, and facilitating their transition back into civilian life. Known for its comprehensive care approach, WWP has made significant strides in supporting veterans.

- **Financial Efficiency**: Approximately 71% of WWP's budget is spent directly on programs for veterans, with a strong emphasis on mental health support, physical health and wellness, and economic empowerment.
- **Impact**: Since its inception, WWP has helped thousands of veterans through direct services, advocacy, and community-building initiatives. Although rocked with scandal a few years back (*chapter*

17), this organization seems to be back on track. That statement now seems overly obvious, since WWP is on this list.

2. Tunnel to Towers Foundation: Founded in memory of firefighter Stephen Siller, who died on 9/11, Tunnel to Towers provides mortgage-free homes to families of fallen first responders and severely injured veterans. Their commitment to ensuring these heroes and their families are taken care of has made a significant impact on many lives.

- **Financial Efficiency**: Over 93% of Tunnel to Towers' budget goes directly to its programs, making it one of the most efficient charities.
- **Impact**: The foundation has built and delivered dozens of smart homes to injured veterans, providing them with independence and security.

3. Direct Relief Direct Relief provides medical assistance to improve the health and lives of people affected by poverty and emergencies. They focus on disaster response, maternal and child health, and disease prevention.

- **Financial Efficiency**: Direct Relief spends about 99% of its budget on program services.
- **Impact**: Their efforts have delivered millions of dollars in medical supplies and support to disaster-stricken areas around the world.

4. Feeding America Feeding America is the nation's largest domestic hunger-relief organization, working through a network of food banks to distribute food to those in need.

- **Financial Efficiency**: Feeding America spends about 98% of its budget on programs. It is praised for its efficiency and impact in addressing food insecurity.
- **Impact**: The organization provides over 6 billion meals annually to those in need.

5. St. Jude Children's Research Hospital Founded in 1962, St. Jude leads research and treatment of pediatric catastrophic diseases. Families never receive a bill for treatment, travel, housing, or food.

- **Financial Efficiency**: St. Jude spends approximately 82% of its budget on research and patient care.
- **Impact**: St. Jude's groundbreaking research has led to treatments that have significantly increased childhood cancer survival rates.

6. The Rotary Foundation The Rotary Foundation supports efforts to promote peace, fight disease, provide clean water and sanitation, support education, and grow local economies.

- **Financial Efficiency**: Around 92% of funds are spent on program services.
- **Impact**: The foundation has been instrumental in efforts to eradicate polio worldwide.

7. The Nature Conservancy Since 1951, The Nature Conservancy has worked to conserve the lands and waters on which all life depends. It works on acquiring land, promoting sustainable practices, and forming conservation easements with communities.

- **Financial Efficiency**: The Nature Conservancy spends approximately 76% of its budget on conservation programs.
- **Impact**: The Conservancy's work in preserving the Amazon rainforest has helped protect millions of acres of vital ecosystems.

8. Médecins Sans Frontières (Doctors Without Borders) Founded in 1971, Médecins Sans Frontières provides medical care in conflict zones and areas affected by disease outbreaks.

- **Financial Efficiency**: MSF spends around 85% of its budget on program activities.
- **Impact**: MSF's rapid response to the Ebola outbreak in West Africa

saved thousands of lives and helped contain the epidemic.

9. UNICEF UNICEF works in over 190 countries and territories to save children's lives, defend their rights, and help them fulfill their potential.

- **Financial Efficiency**: UNICEF spends about 88% of its budget on programs for children.
- **Impact**: UNICEF's vaccination programs have significantly reduced child mortality rates worldwide.

10. Habitat for Humanity Founded in 1976, Habitat for Humanity builds and renovates affordable housing for families in need.

- **Financial Efficiency**: Habitat for Humanity allocates about 77% of its budget to program services.
- **Impact**: Through their global village program, Habitat for Humanity has built and improved housing for over 29 million people.

Case Studies
Wounded Warrior Project: The Warrior Care Network
WWP's Warrior Care Network is an amazing program that works with top medical centers to offer specialized mental health care for veterans. This network provides helpful programs for treating combat-related mental health issues like PTSD, and you don't need to be in a hospital. Veterans who complete the program see big improvements in their quality of life, showing that WWP's work really makes a difference.

Tunnel to Towers: Smart Home Program
The Smart Home Program by Tunnel to Towers is a remarkable example of charity productivity. These homes are specifically made for veterans with severe injuries, and have automated systems to help them be more independent. Marine Corporal Todd Nicely, who lost all four limbs in Afghanistan, received a home that he can control using a tablet. This has greatly improved his daily life, allowing him to control lights, temperature, and security features.

Direct Relief: Hurricane Maria Response

CHARITY GIVING DONATION REVELATION

Direct Relief swiftly helped Puerto Rico after Hurricane Maria by giving medical supplies and aid. They effectively delivered over $70 million worth of medicines and supplies, restoring medical services on the island.

Feeding America: COVID-19 Response

Feeding America worked harder during the COVID-19 pandemic to tackle food insecurity. The organization worked with food banks and distributed millions of extra meals to those affected by the pandemic.

St. Jude Children's Research Hospital: Immunotherapy Research

St. Jude's research in immunotherapy led to new treatments for childhood cancers that were once thought to be untreatable. These advancements helped the hospital save more children with cancer.

Useless Helpful Tidbits

- **Metrics Used to Measure Charity Productivity**: Common metrics include the program expense ratio (percentage of total expenses spent on programs), fundraising efficiency (amount spent to raise $1), and the impact per dollar spent.
- **Records of the Highest-Impact Initiatives**: The Bill and Melinda Gates Foundation's polio eradication efforts have significantly reduced polio cases worldwide, demonstrating high-impact philanthropy.
- **Inspiring Stories from Productive Charities**: The story of Tunnel to Towers Foundation helping the family of NYPD officer Rafael Ramos, who was killed in the line of duty, by paying off their mortgage, exemplifies the immediate and life-changing impact productive charities can have.
- **The Great Charity Ice Bucket Challenge**: Remember the Ice Bucket Challenge that took social media by storm in 2014? It raised over $115 million for ALS research, significantly boosting awareness and funding for the disease. The campaign's success is a testament to the power of viral fundraising and creative charity initiatives.
- **When a Single Story Makes a World of Difference**: In 1984, BBC's broadcast of the Ethiopian famine led to the creation of Band Aid and the Live Aid concerts, raising over $125 million for famine relief.

The initiative showed that a single powerful story can inspire people all over the world to support and donate resources. The power of media-driven philanthropy proved itself.

These effective charities show how donations can make a real and lasting difference. Philanthropy is the forefront of these organizations. Either they directly assist people or they contribute to significant public health projects.

Chapter 4: Evaluating Charities Before You Donate

Importance of Research

Before you reach for your wallet, let's take a moment to talk about the fine art of charitable giving. Now, donating to charity is a noble endeavor, akin to being a modern-day Robin Hood, but without the archery lessons and questionable fashion choices. However, unlike our medieval hero, you need to be a bit more discerning about where your hard-earned money goes.

Research is your best friend here. Think of it as a treasure hunt, but instead of gold coins, you're searching for trustworthy organizations that will use your donations wisely. Not all charities are created equal, and some are more like the Sheriff of Nottingham, misusing funds and engaging in nefarious activities. Yes, a few rotten apples exist in the world of goodwill.

But fear not! By donning your detective hat and doing a little sleuthing, you can dodge the dubious and support the stellar. Check for transparency reports, financial statements, and reviews from fellow do-gooders. Websites like Charity Navigator, GuideStar, and the Better Business Bureau's Wise Giving Alliance are great places to start.

Remember, a well-researched donation is a powerful thing. It ensures your contributions actually reach those in need and make a tangible difference. So, channel your inner Sherlock, do your homework, and donate with confidence. Your wallet, and the world, will thank you!

How to Research

1. Check Financial Health

- **Charity Navigator**: Provides ratings based on financial health, accountability, and transparency.
- **GuideStar**: Offers comprehensive data on nonprofit organizations, including financial statements and impact reports.
- **BBB Wise Giving Alliance**: Evaluates charities based on 20 standards of accountability.

2. Review Transparency and Accountability

- Look for detailed financial reports and annual reports on the charity's website.
- Ensure the charity has clear policies on governance, ethical standards, and conflict of interest.

3. Assess Impact and Outcomes

- Examine the charity's mission and goals to see if they align with your values.
- Look for evidence of measurable outcomes and tangible impacts from the charity's programs.

4. Verify Legitimacy

- Confirm the charity is registered with the appropriate regulatory bodies.
- Check for accreditation from reputable watchdog organizations.

5. Read Reviews and Testimonials

- Look for reviews from other donors and beneficiaries.
- Consult third-party reviews and independent evaluations.

Red Flags
1. Lack of Transparency

- Absence of detailed financial reports or annual reports.
- Vague or overly broad mission statements.

2. High Administrative Costs

- A significant portion of the budget spent on administrative expenses rather than programs.

3. Aggressive Fundraising Tactics

- Pressure to donate immediately or provide personal financial information.

4. Unverifiable Claims

- Grandiose claims about impact without evidence or data to back them up.

5. Poor Governance

- Lack of a clear governance structure or accountability measures.

Useless Helpful Tidbits
1. Famous Charity Scams

- **United Way Scandal**: In the early 1990s, the United Way of America was rocked by a scandal involving its president, William Aramony, who was convicted of fraud and financial mismanagement.
- **Cancer Fund of America**: The organization and its affiliates were shut down in 2015 after being exposed for misusing millions of dollars intended for cancer patients.

2. Tips from Expert Donors

- **Warren Buffett**: Recommends focusing on the charity's effectiveness and the measurable impact of their work.
- **Oprah Winfrey**: Advises giving to causes you are passionate about and ensuring the charity is transparent and accountable.

3. Surprising Sources of Charitable Ratings

- **CharityWatch**: Provides detailed ratings and analysis of nonprofit organizations based on rigorous standards.
- **GreatNonprofits**: A platform where donors and volunteers can leave reviews and ratings for charities, providing a grassroots perspective on

performance and impact.

Before you become a philanthropic force, let's discuss the crucial task of researching charities. Picture yourself as a savvy investor, but instead of stocks and bonds, you're dealing in kindness and goodwill. By taking the time to dive into the world of charitable organizations, you can ensure that your donations are more impactful than a superhero landing.

Thorough research is your trusty sidekick in this endeavor. It helps you sidestep the villainous scams that lurk in the shadows, waiting to snatch your generosity for less-than-noble causes. Yes, even in the realm of charity, there are a few tricksters who prefer lining their own pockets to helping those in need. But fear not! By investigating, you can easily identify these troublemakers.

Start by checking out transparency reports, financial statements, and reviews from other donors. Websites like Charity Navigator, GuideStar, and the Better Business Bureau's Wise Giving Alliance are your go-to sources for this intel. It's like having a magnifying glass that reveals the true nature of these organizations.

If you carefully evaluate charities, you can make sure your donations are being used effectively. Instead, they're fueling the missions of organizations that are actually making a difference. So, embrace your inner sleuth, dig into the details, and give with the confidence that your money is going exactly where it's needed most.

Chapter 5: Making the Most of Your Donations

Maximizing Impact

To ensure your donations make the biggest difference, consider the following strategies:

1. Focus on High-Impact Organizations

- Prioritize charities that demonstrate measurable outcomes and have a proven track record of effectiveness. Use tools like Charity Navigator, GuideStar, and GiveWell to identify high-impact organizations.

2. Give Unrestricted Funds

- While it can be tempting to specify how your donation should be used, unrestricted funds give charities the flexibility to allocate resources where they are most needed.

3. Consider Recurring Donations

- Monthly or annual donations provide charities with a stable and predictable source of income, allowing them to plan and execute long-term projects more effectively.

4. Pool Resources with Others

- Joining or forming a giving circle allows you to pool your resources with others, increasing your collective impact and supporting larger projects or initiatives.

5. Support Underfunded Causes

- Consider donating to causes that receive less attention and funding but are equally important. These can include smaller charities or niche issues that align with your values.

Matching Donations

Many employers offer matching gift programs, where they match the charitable contributions made by their employees. Here's how to leverage matching gifts:

1. Check Your Employer's Policy

- Inquire whether your employer has a matching gift program and understand the terms, including the maximum amount matched and the types of eligible charities.

2. Submit Matching Gift Requests

- Follow your employer's procedures for submitting matching gift requests. This typically involves filling out a form and providing proof of your donation.

3. Encourage Others

- Inform colleagues and friends about matching gift opportunities to maximize collective impact.

4. Use Matching Gift Tools

- Websites like Double the Donation and Benevity can help you identify matching gift opportunities and streamline the submission process.

Volunteering and In-Kind Donations

Contributing your time and skills or donating goods can be just as valuable as financial donations:

1. Volunteering

- Offer your professional skills, such as legal advice, graphic design, or marketing, to charities in need of expertise.
- Participate in hands-on activities like building homes, tutoring, or organizing community events.

2. In-Kind Donations

- Donate items such as clothing, food, medical supplies, and technology equipment.
- Check with charities to determine their current needs and ensure your in-kind donations are useful.

3. Organize Drives

- Host donation drives for items like school supplies, hygiene kits, or non-perishable food.

Useless Helpful Tidbits

- **Ice Bucket Challenge**: This viral social media campaign raised over $115 million for ALS research by encouraging people to dump ice water over their heads and challenge others to donate.
- **Warren Buffett's Lunch Auction**: Each year, Warren Buffett auctions off a lunch date with him, raising millions for the Glide Foundation, which supports homeless and low-income individuals.
- **Cryptocurrency Donations**: Some charities now accept Bitcoin and other cryptocurrencies, providing a new way for tech-savvy donors to contribute.
- **Airline Miles**: Organizations like Make-A-Wish accept donated frequent flyer miles to help grant wishes for children with critical illnesses.
- **Wedding Dresses**: Brides Across America collects wedding dresses and gives them to military brides in need.
- **Cars**: Many charities, including the American Cancer Society and Habitat for Humanity, accept donated vehicles to fund their programs.
- **Prom Dresses**: Programs like Operation Prom collect and distribute prom dresses to underprivileged high school students.

You can make a big difference by using these strategies and finding creative ways to give. Whether through financial donations, volunteering, or in-kind gifts, every act of generosity counts.

Chapter 6: The Future of Charitable Giving

Welcome to the futuristic realm of charitable giving, where technology meets altruism, and innovation paves the way for impactful philanthropy. Imagine your donations flying through the internet like a speedy owl from Harry Potter. As we dive into the future, we'll explore how emerging trends, global events, and sustainable practices are reshaping the way we give. Picture an exciting adventure in the realm of giving, with digital wallets, AI-driven fundraisers, and a sprinkle of eco-friendly enchantment. So, buckle up, adjust your virtual reality goggles, and let's embark on this exciting journey!

Trends and Innovations

In the ever-evolving world of charitable giving, new trends and innovations are emerging at a breakneck pace. Imagine trying to keep up with the Kardashians but in the world of philanthropy! Here's a look at some of the most transformative developments:

1. Digital Donations and Cryptocurrencies Charities are increasingly accepting digital currencies like Bitcoin, Ethereum, and others, providing a new avenue for tech-savvy donors. No more digging around for loose change or writing checks—now you can donate faster than you can say "blockchain." This technology ensures transparency and security, making it easier for donors to track how their contributions are used. It's like having a charity ledger that even your dog can't bury in the backyard!

2. Social Media Fundraising Platforms like Facebook, Instagram, and Twitter have become powerful tools for raising awareness and funds. Gone are the days of bake sales and car washes (though we do love a good brownie!). Now, viral campaigns, crowdfunding, and peer-to-peer fundraising enable charities to reach a broader audience and mobilize resources quicker than you can share a cat meme. Just imagine: one tweet about your favorite cause could spread like wildfire, turning "likes" into lifesaving donations.

3. AI and Data Analytics Artificial Intelligence (AI) and data analytics are revolutionizing how charities operate. These technologies help organizations predict donor behavior, optimize fundraising strategies, and measure impact more effectively. It's like having a crystal ball that also gives great financial advice. AI can tell you when donors are most likely to give, what messages will resonate best, and even predict future trends in giving. So, charities can now spend less time guessing and more time making a real difference.

By embracing these innovations, the world of charitable giving is becoming more efficient, engaging, and downright futuristic. So, whether you're a digital currency enthusiast, a social media maven, or a data geek, there's a way for you to make a positive impact like never before. Donating has never been so high-tech and fun—it's practically philanthropy 2.0!

4. Virtual and Augmented Reality

Virtual and augmented reality offer immersive experiences that can engage donors in new ways. Imagine touring a village that needs clean water or seeing firsthand the impact of your donation in a remote school—all from the comfort of your home.

5. Mobile Giving

With the ubiquity of smartphones, mobile giving has become incredibly popular. Text-to-donate campaigns and mobile apps make it easier than ever for people to contribute to their favorite causes.

Impact of Global Events

Global events such as pandemics, natural disasters, and economic crises significantly influence charitable giving patterns. Here's how:

1. Pandemics

The COVID-19 pandemic highlighted the critical role of charities in providing relief and support. As the world turned upside down and everyone collectively asked, "Is 2020 over yet?" donations surged like never before. Individuals and corporations rallied to support healthcare, food security, and economic relief efforts. It was like everyone suddenly discovered their inner superhero—minus the capes, but with plenty of masks.

The pandemic also accelerated the adoption of digital fundraising methods. In a world where we couldn't even meet up for a cup of coffee, technology became our lifeline. Virtual galas, online auctions, and crowdfunding campaigns took center stage. Forget the old-fashioned bake sales; now you could fundraise in your pajamas while binge-watching your favorite shows.

Charities got creative too. Remember that time when people were doing push-ups and ice bucket challenges for a cause? The pandemic brought forth a new wave of innovative fundraising ideas. There were virtual 5Ks where you could run around your living room, live-streamed concerts featuring your favorite bands playing from their garages, and even Zoom charity events where you could bid on items without worrying about anyone seeing your poker face.

But it wasn't all fun and games—okay, it was mostly fun and games, but there was some serious impact happening too. Donations were used to support healthcare by providing hospitals with essential PPE and ventilators. People joined together to help food banks and meal delivery services, which greatly helped improve food security programs for those affected by the economic downturn.

Economic relief efforts also got a much-needed injection of funds. Charities played a crucial role in helping small businesses and individuals affected by the pandemic's economic impact.

Act included even big corporations. Famous companies made large donations, matching what their employees gave and creating their own funds to help. It was like a corporate version of "Oprah's Favorite Things," but instead of giving away cars, they were giving away hope and support.

In summary, the COVID-19 pandemic might have put the world on pause, but it certainly pressed fast-forward on the evolution of charitable giving. Digital fundraising methods became the new norm, and the spirit of giving proved to be more contagious than any virus. Although we're eager to move on from 2020, the lessons and innovations from the pandemic will still impact philanthropy's future.

2. Natural Disasters

Just as receiving a surprise pizza makes us happy, natural disasters also prompt people to donate generously right away. Organizations like the Red Cross and Doctors Without Borders respond quickly to provide aid during disasters. These organizations are like the superheroes of the charity world, swooping in with supplies, medical care, and a whole lot of hope.

Social media and crowdfunding have become their trusty sidekicks in these efforts. Remember the days when charity appeals were limited to phone-a-thons and snail mail? With internet power, fundraising is just a tweet away. One viral post can reach millions, turning "likes" into life-saving donations. It's like having a virtual megaphone that never runs out of batteries.

When disaster strikes, these organizations leverage social media to spread the word and rally support. You might see your favorite celebrities sharing donation links, or a touching story about a rescue operation going viral. The photos of volunteers in action are heartwarming, often with hashtags like #DisasterRelief and #WeGotThis.

Crowdfunding platforms also play a crucial role. Sites like GoFundMe and JustGiving enable people from all over the world to contribute to relief efforts. It's like passing the hat around at a giant, global concert—only instead of tipping the band, you're helping to rebuild communities. People's generosity can be truly amazing when it comes to campaigns for emergency supplies, medical aid, or rebuilding efforts.

Organizations such as the Red Cross and Médecins Sans Frontières are experts at this. They know how to harness the power of social media to keep the public informed and engaged. Donors are kept informed through regular updates, compelling stories, and transparent financial reports. It's like watching a real-time superhero movie, where every donation is a plot twist that brings hope and relief to those in need.

Natural disasters can cause chaos and destruction, but they also show how people can come together and help each other. Thanks to social media and crowdfunding, organizations can now raise funds and provide aid more quickly and efficiently. So next time you see a post about a disaster relief effort, remember that even a small contribution can make a big difference. And who knows, you might just be the next unsung hero in the ongoing saga of global goodwill.

3. Economic Crises

Economic downturns impact charitable giving in various ways, similar to receiving socks for your birthday - some may not prefer them, while others find them useful. When the economy takes a nosedive, some donors may tighten their belts and cut back on their contributions. It's understandable; after all, when your wallet feels lighter than a feather, discretionary spending on anything, including charity, can seem daunting.

However, economic hardships can also ignite a spark of generosity in others. For some, witnessing widespread need prompts a desire to help, even if it means sacrificing a little more of their own comfort. These compassionate souls dig deep, increasing their contributions to support those who are hit hardest by the downturn. It's like a scene from a holiday movie where the grumpy neighbor ends up donating his entire Christmas bonus to the local orphanage.

Charities, on their part, must be as nimble as a cat in a room full of rocking chairs to navigate these challenging times. They need to adapt their strategies to ensure they can still fulfill their missions despite financial constraints. This might mean ramping up their storytelling game to highlight the urgent need and impact of donations. After all, a heartwarming story can open wallets faster than you can say "tax deduction."

Additionally, charities might explore new fundraising avenues. Virtual events, online auctions, and creative campaigns can help bridge the gap when traditional donations wane. Think of it as switching from selling lemonade at a stand to offering it through a nationwide lemonade subscription box service. It's all about finding innovative ways to connect with donors.

Economic downturns also push charities to emphasize the importance of every donation, no matter how small. They could run campaigns that highlight the impact of small donations, showing how even small contributions can make a big difference. It's like those moments in movies where everyone chips in their spare change to save the community center; it adds up and makes a significant difference.

Finally, transparency and communication become even more crucial. Donors want to know that their contributions are being used wisely, especially when every dollar counts more than ever. Sharing regular updates, thorough reports, and clear impact statements builds trust and keeps support going.

Economic downturns can dampen charitable giving, but they can also inspire great generosity. Charities that are adaptable, transparent, and use impactful stories can still thrive during difficult times. Economic slumps reveal people's resilience, offering hope and opportunities for change.

Sustainability and Long-Term Impact

Ensuring sustainable giving practices and long-term impact is crucial for the future of charitable giving. Here are some strategies to achieve this:

1. Focus on Local Communities

Supporting local initiatives can ensure that funds are used effectively and that projects are sustainable. Local organizations often have a better understanding of the community's needs and can implement solutions that have lasting impacts.

2. Promote Transparency and Accountability

Transparency and accountability are key to building trust with donors. Charities must provide clear reports on how donations are used and the impact they achieve. This encourages ongoing support and sustainable funding.

3. Encourage Recurring Donations

Regular donations provide stable income for charities, making it easier for them to plan and execute long-term projects. Monthly giving programs are an excellent way to cultivate donor loyalty and sustain support.

4. Invest in Capacity Building

Charities should invest in their infrastructure and capacity to ensure they can deliver on their promises. This includes staff training, technological upgrades, and developing robust systems for monitoring and evaluation.

Useless Helpful Tidbits

1. **Charity Robots:** Automated helpers for logistical support in disaster zones.
2. **Smart Contracts:** Blockchain-based contracts that release funds automatically when specific conditions are met.
3. **Virtual Volunteering:** Using avatars to participate in charitable activities in virtual reality environments.

Innovative Charities Leading the Way

Charity: Water: Charity: Water is at the forefront of using technology to connect donors with the impact of their contributions. They are using virtual reality (VR) to show donors the communities benefiting from their clean water projects. Picture yourself putting on a VR headset and being transported to a remote village. You'll see the happiness and change that a new well brings. This immersive experience helps donors understand the real impact of their generosity by making the concept of water scarcity feel real and personal. Founded by Scott Harrison in 2006, Charity: Water has funded over 100,000 water projects in 29 countries, bringing clean and safe drinking water to more than 14 million people.

The Ocean Cleanup: The Ocean Cleanup is an innovative nonprofit focused on removing plastic pollution from the world's oceans and rivers. Boyan Slat, a Dutch inventor, founded the organization. They use advanced technology, like floating barriers, to collect plastic waste. Their flagship project targets the Great Pacific Garbage Patch, a notorious accumulation of ocean plastic. By deploying autonomous systems that can operate continuously, The Ocean Cleanup aims to remove 90% of floating ocean plastic by 2040. They've also expanded their efforts to tackle river pollution through their "Interceptor" systems, which prevent plastic from reaching the ocean in the first place. Their commitment to restoring the environment is shown through their approach of cleaning up both oceans and rivers.

GiveDirectly: GiveDirectly is revolutionizing the way we think about charity by leveraging mobile technology to provide direct cash transfers to people living in extreme poverty. Founded in 2009 by four economics graduates, this organization changes the way aid works. They give money directly to people and let them decide how to use it. This approach is because individuals are best placed to understand their own needs. Using mobile money platforms, GiveDirectly can transfer funds quickly and efficiently, reaching recipients in remote areas without the need for costly intermediaries. Rigorous evaluations have shown that direct cash transfers can significantly improve recipients' quality of life, boosting everything from food security to educational opportunities..

Fun Facts About Futuristic Giving Methods

CryptoKitties for Charity: In the whimsical world of blockchain, even digital cats can make a difference! CryptoKitties, those adorable, virtual feline collectibles that took the internet by storm, are not just for fun—they can also be a force for good. These digital collectibles, along with other NFTs (non-fungible tokens), are being auctioned off to raise funds for various charitable causes. Picture yourself adopting a virtual kitty that supports clean water, disaster relief, and education for kids in need. It's like having a pet that never needs feeding or litter changes, but still manages to change the world.

CryptoKitties collaborated with organizations to auction exclusive kitties and donated the proceeds to charity. This trend has expanded to other NFTs as well, where artists and creators mint unique digital art pieces that are sold to benefit causes they care about. The use of advanced technology and digital ownership is changing how we do philanthropy. Next time you see a pixelated cat or digital artwork being sold for a lot of money, remember that it's a cute and creative way to make a positive difference.

Wearable Donation Devices: Who knew that breaking a sweat could also break the cycle of poverty or fund medical research? Discover wearable devices that turn your workouts into donations for charity. It's like having a personal trainer and philanthropist rolled into one stylish wrist accessory.

Here's how it works: These devices track your steps, calories burned, or miles run, and convert them into donations to your chosen charity. Companies partner with health-focused apps and nonprofits to pledge funds based on the user's activity levels. Every mile or step you take can help support causes like fighting hunger, cancer research, and protecting endangered species. It's the ultimate win-win situation: you get fitter, and the world becomes a better place.

Some programs even gamify the experience, offering challenges and milestones that unlock additional donations. Imagine earning extra charity bucks for completing a 5K run or hitting your daily step goal for a month straight. It's like leveling up in a video game, but instead of virtual rewards, you're making a tangible difference in the real world.

Wearable donation devices make giving back easy, fun, and promote physical activity for important causes. Every step brings us closer to improved health and a better world.

AI-Generated Art: Welcome to the intersection of art, technology, and philanthropy, where even computers have a creative streak! AI-generated art is becoming a unique and exciting way to support charitable organizations. Imagine an AI system that learns from many artworks and creates its own masterpieces, just as good as those made by humans. These digital artworks are then sold at auctions, with the proceeds going to various charitable causes.

The concept is as futuristic as it gets. AI algorithms use art history to create unique and mind-blowing pieces of art. These AI-created pieces are then put up for auction, drawing in collectors and philanthropists eager to own a slice of cutting-edge creativity while supporting good causes. It's like having a robot Picasso whose earnings go straight to charity.

A famous example is the sale of an AI-created artwork called "Edmond de Belamy" by the French art group Obvious. It sold for a whopping $432,500 in an auction. Proceeds from similar sales have supported educational programs, environmental initiatives, and health-related research. AI art is not just interesting because it's new.

CHARITY GIVING DONATION REVELATION

AI art auctions have two advantages: they push creative boundaries with technology and raise funds for important causes. Unconventional signature in digital artwork might be the latest trend in improving the world.

As we move forward, it's evident that charitable giving will change due to technology, global issues, and people's generous nature. By embracing these trends and innovations, we can ensure that our contributions make a meaningful and lasting impact on the world.

Chapter 7: Personal Stories of Giving

Join us on a journey of giving, where we share personal stories of people making a difference. These stories show how generosity can make a big difference and offer wisdom from experienced donors. To top it off, we'll sprinkle in some inspirational quotes and a dash of quirky, fun facts about famous philanthropists.

Heartwarming Stories

1. The Tale of Sarah's Scholarship Fund

Sarah, a high school teacher, was deeply moved by the struggles of her students who couldn't afford college. Determined to make a difference, she started a scholarship fund with her own savings. Over the years, she raised over $100,000, helping dozens of students achieve their dreams of higher education. One of her beneficiaries, now a successful engineer, continues to pay it forward by contributing to the fund annually.

2. John and the Community Playground

John, a retired carpenter, noticed that the local park's playground was in disrepair. Using his carpentry skills, he began fixing the equipment with donated materials. His initiative caught the community's attention, and soon, volunteers and donations poured in. Today, the playground stands as a testament to John's selflessness, providing joy to countless children.

3. Emma's Animal Rescue Mission

Emma, an animal lover, turned her home into a rescue center for abandoned pets. She started with just a few animals but quickly expanded, using social media to raise awareness and funds. Her rescue mission grew into a full-fledged non-profit, re-homing over 500 pets and advocating for animal welfare in her community.

Lessons Learned

1. Start Small but Dream Big

Many experienced donors emphasize the importance of starting with what you can afford, whether it's time, money, or skills. Small contributions can lead to significant impacts over time, especially when they inspire others to join the cause.

2. Transparency Builds Trust

Donors who have been most successful stress the importance of transparency. Being open about where funds go and the impact they achieve not only builds trust but also encourages more donations.

3. Stay Passionate and Persistent

Passion for the cause keeps the momentum going, even when challenges arise. Persistence is key, as long-term impact often requires sustained effort and commitment.

Inspiring Children's Charities

In this segment, we focus on charities that help children with serious illnesses and challenges in their lives. These organizations make a big difference in the lives of young patients and their families by bringing hope, joy, and important support. Let's examine the achievements and challenges of two famous charities, Make-A-Wish Foundation and Give Kids The World Village.

Make-A-Wish Foundation

The Make-A-Wish Foundation is renowned for granting life-changing wishes to children with critical illnesses. Founded in 1980, the organization has grown significantly, now operating in nearly 50 countries. Make-A-Wish grants the dreams of kids with serious medical conditions to bring hope, strength, and joy to them and their families.

Positive Impact: Make-A-Wish has granted over 500,000 wishes globally, each tailored to the child's unique desires, whether it's meeting a celebrity, going on a dream vacation, or receiving a special gift. The children and their families receive emotional benefits and a respite from the challenges of coping with a serious illness. Studies have shown that wish experiences can improve the quality of life and even contribute to better health outcomes.

Criticisms and Challenges: While the foundation's mission is widely praised, Make-A-Wish has faced some criticism regarding the allocation of funds. Some people think it's better to use donations for granting wishes instead of administrative and fundraising costs. However, the organization maintains that these expenses are necessary to sustain its operations and expand its reach. Overall, Make-A-Wish is generally regarded positively, with most donations effectively contributing to its mission.

Give Kids The World Village

Give Kids The World Village is a charity resort in Florida that offers free vacations to sick children and their families. Since 1986, the resort has been giving away a week-long vacation package for free. It includes accommodation, meals, and tickets to theme parks like Walt Disney World and Universal Studios.

Positive Impact: The impact of Give Kids The World Village is significant, having hosted over 175,000 families from all over the world. The resort creates a magical experience for children who are often unable to enjoy typical family vacations due to medical and financial constraints. The village works with wish-granting organizations and donors to make sure every family has an incredible vacation.

Criticisms and Challenges: While Give Kids The World Village receives widespread acclaim, it too faces challenges in maintaining transparency and efficiency in fund allocation. Critics argue that running a large-scale operation is expensive due to facility maintenance and coordinating volunteers. Despite these concerns, the organization is generally well-regarded for its dedication to providing joyous experiences for children with critical illnesses.

Inspirational Quotes

- "The best way to find yourself is to lose yourself in the service of others." – **Mahatma Gandhi**
- "No one has ever become poor by giving." – **Anne Frank**
- "It's not how much we give, but how much love we put into giving." – **Mother Teresa**
- "The meaning of life is to find your gift. The purpose of life is to give it away." – **Pablo Picasso**

Useless Helpful Tidbits

1. **Andrew Carnegie:** Donated over $350 million (equivalent to billions today) to libraries, education, and peace initiatives.
2. **Bill and Melinda Gates:** Through the Bill & Melinda Gates Foundation, they have given over $50 billion to global health, development, and education.

3. **Warren Buffett:** Committed to giving away 99% of his fortune, he has donated billions to the Gates Foundation and other charities.
4. **Oprah Winfrey:** Built the Oprah Winfrey Leadership Academy for Girls in South Africa, inspired by her own struggles with education growing up.
5. **Chuck Feeney:** The co-founder of Duty-Free Shoppers, Feeney secretly gave away his fortune of over $8 billion, living a life of frugality in the process.
6. **JK Rowling:** Lost her billionaire status because she donated so much to charity, including her own charitable trust, Volant.
7. **Anonymous Angel in Australia:** For years, an anonymous donor known as the "Good Samaritan" has been leaving $100,000 checks in the mailboxes of struggling families and community organizations across Australia.
8. **The Secret Santa of Kansas City:** Each year, a businessman goes around Kansas City handing out $100 bills to random strangers, often targeting those who seem to be in need, spreading holiday cheer and hope.
9. **Pizza Delivery Surprise:** In 2020, a pizza delivery driver in Massachusetts received a $2,020 tip from a group of friends who wanted to support local workers during the pandemic. The driver, a single mother, was overwhelmed with gratitude and used the money to pay off bills and buy gifts for her children.

These stories show how individual generosity can make a big difference, inspiring others and changing lives. The future of charitable giving offers heartwarming stories, lessons, and fun facts for everyone to enjoy. Spread kindness to make the world better.

Chapter 8: The Psychology of Giving

Explore the psychology of giving, uncovering why people donate and how it benefits them. Get ready to learn about the science of generosity with fascinating studies, intriguing facts, and surprising statistics.

Motivations Behind Charitable Giving

Charitable giving is a complex behavior influenced by various psychological factors. Here's a look at some key motivators:

1. Empathy and Compassion

Empathy is a powerful driver of charitable giving. When individuals see others in distress, they often feel a strong emotional connection that compels them to help. Compassionate responses are heightened when people can vividly imagine the suffering of others or see themselves in similar situations.

2. Social Influence

Social norms and peer pressure significantly impact giving behavior. People are more likely to donate if they see others around them doing so. Fundraising events, social media campaigns, and public recognition can all boost donations by leveraging social influence.

3. Personal Values and Beliefs

Personal values, such as a sense of justice, equality, or religious beliefs, strongly motivate charitable actions. Many individuals donate to causes that align with their moral or ethical values, seeking to make a difference in areas they deeply care about.

4. Reciprocity

The principle of reciprocity—the desire to give back when one has received something—plays a crucial role in charitable giving. This can be seen in scenarios where individuals donate to organizations from which they or their loved ones have benefited.

5. Personal Satisfaction and Joy

The "warm glow" effect refers to the positive feelings people experience when they give. This emotional reward can be a powerful motivator, as people seek the satisfaction and happiness that comes from helping others.

Altruism vs. Self-Interest

Charitable giving often involves a blend of altruism and self-interest. Let's explore this balance:

1. Pure Altruism

Altruistic giving is motivated by a genuine desire to help others without expecting anything in return. This type of giving is driven by empathy, compassion, and a selfless concern for the well-being of others.

2. Impure Altruism

Impure altruism involves giving that, while still benefiting others, also provides some form of reward to the donor. This could be emotional satisfaction, social recognition, or even tax benefits. The blend of selflessness and self-interest makes this type of giving common.

3. Egoistic Giving

Egoistic giving is primarily driven by self-interest, where the donor's primary motivation is personal gain. This could include enhancing one's reputation, gaining social status, or receiving tangible rewards. While the end result is still beneficial to the recipient, the donor's motivations are largely self-serving.

Impact of Giving on Donors

Charitable giving not only benefits recipients but also has profound positive effects on donors. Here's how:

1. Mental and Emotional Well-being

Studies have shown that giving can reduce stress, increase happiness, and enhance overall well-being. The act of helping others triggers the release of endorphins, leading to what is often referred to as the "helper's high."

2. Sense of Purpose and Fulfillment

Donating to meaningful causes can provide a sense of purpose and fulfillment. Knowing that one's contributions are making a positive impact can boost self-esteem and life satisfaction.

3. Social Connections

Charitable activities often involve social interaction, which can lead to stronger community ties and social networks. Volunteering, participating in fundraising events, and engaging with charitable organizations can help donors feel more connected and supported.

CHARITY GIVING DONATION REVELATION

Useless Helpful Tidbits

1. **The Dictator Game:** A popular experiment in behavioral economics, the Dictator Game reveals that people often choose to share their resources even when there is no obligation to do so, highlighting inherent tendencies toward generosity.
2. **Neuroimaging Studies:** Research using fMRI scans shows that the brain's reward centers are activated when individuals donate to charity, similar to the response seen when receiving a reward.

Fun Facts About Why People Give

1. **The Power of Stories:** People are more likely to donate when they hear a compelling personal story rather than when they are presented with statistics. This is known as the "identifiable victim effect."
2. **Mood Booster:** Acts of kindness, including charitable donations, can boost the donor's mood for hours or even days, contributing to overall mental health.

Interesting Statistics on Donor Behavior

1. **Generational Giving:** Millennials are more likely to donate through online platforms and social media campaigns, while Baby Boomers tend to prefer traditional methods such as mailing checks.
2. **Gender Differences:** Studies have shown that women are generally more likely to donate than men and often give more to causes related to health and social services.
3. **Impact of Income:** Surprisingly, lower-income individuals tend to give a higher percentage of their income to charity compared to higher-income individuals, possibly driven by a stronger sense of empathy and community.
4. **Workplace Giving Programs:** Workplace giving programs are a significant driver of charitable donations. Companies often match employee donations dollar for dollar, effectively doubling the impact of each contribution. Research shows that nearly 65% of Fortune 500

companies offer matching gift programs, and employees who participate in these programs donate an average of $2,400 more annually than those who don't. These programs not only boost overall charitable contributions but also foster a culture of generosity within the workplace.

5. **Recurring Donations**: Subscription-style giving is on the rise, with more donors opting for monthly contributions instead of one-time donations. About 45% of donors worldwide are enrolled in recurring giving programs, which provide a steady stream of income for charities. This model not only offers financial stability to nonprofits but also allows donors to integrate philanthropy seamlessly into their monthly budgets. It's like having a Netflix subscription, but instead of streaming shows, you're streaming support to your favorite causes.

As we've explored, the psychology of giving is a rich and multifaceted subject. Learning why people donate and how they balance their own needs with helping others can make us better philanthropists. Your generosity changes lives and enriches your own.

Chapter 9: Corporate Social Responsibility (CSR)

Welcome to the world of Corporate Social Responsibility (CSR), where businesses balance profit with purpose. In this chapter, we'll dive into the definition and significance of CSR, explore successful initiatives by well-known companies, and examine the impact of CSR on both business and society. As always, we'll spice things up with some interesting statistics, notable achievements, and quirky fun facts.

Definition and Importance of CSR

Corporate Social Responsibility (CSR) refers to the practices and policies undertaken by corporations to manage their impact on society and the environment. It's not just about following the rules, but also about making a positive impact on the community and reducing harm to the environment.

Why CSR Matters

1. **Enhancing Reputation and Brand Loyalty**

- ○ Companies that actively engage in CSR build a positive image and earn the trust of consumers. This, in turn, fosters brand loyalty and can lead to increased customer retention.

2. **Attracting and Retaining Talent**
   - ○ Employees, particularly millennials and Gen Z, prefer to work for companies that are socially responsible. CSR initiatives can boost employee morale, attract top talent, and reduce turnover rates.

3. **Driving Innovation**
   - ○ CSR encourages businesses to develop sustainable products and processes. This focus on innovation can lead to the creation of new markets and improved operational efficiencies.

4. **Risk Management**
   - ○ By addressing social and environmental issues, companies can mitigate risks associated with negative publicity, regulatory changes, and consumer boycotts.

5. **Positive Social and Environmental Impact**
   - ○ Ultimately, CSR helps companies contribute to the well-being of society and the environment, fostering sustainable development and community growth.

Examples of CSR Initiatives
Patagonia
Environmental Stewardship

- Patagonia is renowned for its commitment to environmental sustainability. The company donates 1% of its sales to environmental causes and actively works to reduce its carbon footprint. Its "Worn Wear" program encourages customers to buy used products and repair their gear, promoting a circular economy.

TOMS
One for One Model

- TOMS pioneered the "One for One" model, where every pair of shoes purchased results in a pair being donated to a child in need. This initiative has expanded to include eyewear, with each purchase helping to restore sight for individuals through medical treatment and prescription glasses.

Ben & Jerry's
Social and Economic Justice

- Ben & Jerry's integrates social and economic justice into its business model. The company supports various causes, including climate change, fair trade, and LGBTQ+ rights. It sources ingredients from Fairtrade-certified producers and uses its platform to advocate for social change.

Impact of CSR on Business and Society
Benefits for Companies

1. **Enhanced Corporate Reputation**
   - Companies with robust CSR programs often enjoy a better public image, which can lead to increased customer loyalty and higher sales.
2. **Employee Engagement and Productivity**
   - CSR initiatives create a sense of pride and purpose among employees, leading to higher engagement, productivity, and job satisfaction.
3. **Operational Efficiencies and Cost Savings**
   - Sustainable practices can reduce waste and energy consumption, leading to significant cost savings over time.

Benefits for Society

1. **Community Development**
   - CSR programs often focus on education, healthcare, and infrastructure development, improving the quality of life in

communities.

2. **Environmental Preservation**
   - ○ Companies that adopt green practices help protect natural resources, reduce pollution, and combat climate change.

3. **Economic Growth**
   - ○ By supporting local suppliers and creating jobs, CSR initiatives contribute to economic development and poverty alleviation.

Useless Helpful Tidbits
Statistics on CSR Effectiveness

1. **Consumer Preferences**
   - ○ A 2020 study by Cone Communications found that 86% of consumers expect companies to address social and environmental issues.

2. **Employee Retention**
   - ○ According to the Society for Human Resource Management, companies with strong sustainability programs experience a 55% improvement in employee morale and a 38% increase in employee loyalty.

Notable CSR Achievements

1. **Microsoft's Carbon Negative Commitment**
   - ○ Microsoft has committed to being carbon negative by 2030 and aims to remove all the carbon it has emitted since its founding by 2050.

2. **Unilever's Sustainable Living Plan**
   - ○ Unilever's plan has helped over a billion people improve their health and well-being and has substantially reduced the company's environmental footprint.

Fun Facts About Quirky CSR Initiatives

1. **The Lego Group's Sustainable Bricks**
   - Lego is investing in developing sustainable bricks made from plant-based materials and recycled plastic, aiming to make all core products from sustainable materials by 2030.
2. **IKEA's Solar Panel Initiative**
   - IKEA not only sells solar panels to its customers but also uses solar energy extensively in its stores, aiming to become energy independent by 2020.
3. **Salesforce's 1-1-1 Philanthropy Model**
   - Salesforce donates 1% of its equity, 1% of its product, and 1% of employees' time to philanthropic causes, demonstrating a comprehensive approach to CSR.

Corporate Social Responsibility is not just a buzzword; it's a powerful approach that benefits both businesses and society. Ethical, innovative, and sustainable companies improve the world. The future of CSR is bright and impactful. It involves protecting the environment, promoting social justice, and innovating giving methods. So, the next time you support a socially responsible company, remember—you're contributing to a larger mission of making the world a better place.

Chapter 10: Grassroots Movements and Small Charities

Explore the world of grassroots movements and small charities, where passion and community spirit make a big impact. This chapter will cover grassroots movements, small charities, and success stories of local heroes. As always, we'll add some fun facts, quirky charities, and inspiring tales of how small efforts can lead to big impacts.

Definition of Grassroots Movements

Grassroots movements are the ultimate underdog story in the world of activism—think of them as the "Rocky Balboa" of social change. These are community-driven initiatives that seek to create change from the ground up, powered by sheer passion and a lot of elbow grease. Picture a determined group of people with handmade signs, a Twitter account, and a strong belief that they can create change. That's the essence of a grassroots movement.

Usually, it's the local heroes, people who care about their community, who step up to tackle social, political, or environmental problems. These are the folks who see a problem in their backyard and decide they're not going to wait around for a knight in shining armor to fix it. Instead, they roll up their sleeves and get to work, rallying their neighbors, friends, and anyone who will listen to join the cause. It's like organizing a block party, but instead of barbecue and lawn games, they're serving up change and civic engagement.

Grassroots movements focus heavily on local involvement. Volunteers are vital to these initiatives, often working with limited resources but endless determination. Picture a group of volunteers at a community clean-up, each armed with a trash bag and a dream of a cleaner neighborhood. Imagine a meeting where residents come together to talk about a new policy proposal, all working together and excited to make a difference for their community.

While these movements may not have a lot of money, they compensate with their creativity and resourcefulness. Grassroots activists are coming up with creative ways to raise money and spread awareness, like bake sales and crowdfunding. They use social media to amplify their message, turning hashtags into battle cries and viral posts into recruitment tools. It's like

MacGyver meets social justice, using everyday tools to achieve extraordinary results.

Humor often plays a role in these movements, too. A witty protest sign can capture attention and spread like wildfire on social media, bringing a light-hearted twist to serious issues. Humor can engage people and spread the word at protests.

In summary, grassroots movements are all about ordinary people doing extraordinary things. They harness the power of community and the drive of passionate individuals to create meaningful change. These movements show that a big impact can be made with little resources, just heart and ingenuity.

Key Characteristics of Grassroots Movements

1. **Local Focus**
   - Grassroots movements are deeply rooted in local issues and work within communities to address them. They prioritize the needs and voices of the people directly affected by the issues.
2. **Community Involvement**
   - These movements rely heavily on the participation and engagement of community members. Volunteers and local leaders play a critical role in driving initiatives forward.
3. **Flexibility and Adaptability**
   - Grassroots movements are often more flexible and adaptable than larger organizations. They can quickly respond to changing circumstances and needs within the community.
4. **Empowerment**
   - Grassroots movements give people the power to make decisions and take action, so they can create the change they desire.

Impact of Small Charities

Even though small charities have fewer resources, they can make a big difference in their communities. Because of their strong ties to the community, they can effectively and creatively address specific needs.

How Small Charities Make a Difference

1. **Targeted Interventions**
    - Small charities can tailor their programs to meet the specific needs of their communities, whether it's providing after-school programs, supporting local food banks, or offering mental health services.
2. **Personalized Support**
    - With a smaller scale, these charities can offer more personalized and direct support to individuals, building stronger relationships and trust.
3. **Community Trust**
    - Being part of the community they serve, small charities often enjoy a higher level of trust and engagement from local residents, which enhances their effectiveness.
4. **Innovation and Creativity**
    - Without the bureaucratic constraints of larger organizations, small charities can implement creative and innovative solutions to address local challenges.

Success Stories

1. The Snowdrop Project

The Snowdrop Project, based in Sheffield, UK, supports survivors of human trafficking. Starting as a small initiative, it provides long-term support, including counseling, legal advice, and skills training. Its holistic approach has transformed the lives of hundreds of survivors, helping them rebuild their lives and integrate into society.

2. Akshaya Patra Foundation

This Indian charity began as a small grassroots effort to provide midday meals to schoolchildren. Today, it is the world's largest nonprofit-run school meal program, serving over 1.8 million children daily across India, significantly improving attendance and educational outcomes.

3. TreePeople

Founded in 1973 by teenager Andy Lipkis, TreePeople started with a group of volunteers planting trees to combat deforestation in Los Angeles. This organization has done a great deal for the environment - they've planted millions of trees, encouraged sustainable urban policies, and engaged thousands of volunteers.

Useless Helpful Tidbits

1. **The Power of Social Media**
   - Social media has become a vital tool for grassroots movements, allowing them to organize, mobilize, and raise awareness quickly. Movements like the Arab Spring and #BlackLivesMatter have shown the global reach and influence of digital activism.

2. **Historical Impact**
   - Many significant social changes have roots in grassroots movements. The Civil Rights Movement and anti-apartheid movement show how grassroots activism can cause big changes in society.

Quirky Small Charities Doing Unique Work

1. **Knitted Knockers**
   - This charity provides handmade, knitted breast prostheses for women who have undergone mastectomies. The soft, comfortable prostheses are made by volunteers and offered free of charge to those in need.

2. **The Library of Things**
   - Based in London, this innovative charity lends out items such as tools, kitchen appliances, and camping gear, promoting a sharing economy and reducing waste. It allows people to borrow rather than buy items they only need occasionally.

3. **Cat Town**
   - Located in Oakland, California, Cat Town focuses on helping at-risk shelter cats find loving homes. It was the first cat café in the U.S. and offers a unique space where potential adopters can interact with cats in a relaxed environment.

CHARITY GIVING DONATION REVELATION

Stories of Big Impacts from Small Efforts

1. **The Be The Match Foundation**
    - Starting as a small initiative, this foundation has grown into a national registry that matches bone marrow donors with patients in need. It has facilitated thousands of life-saving transplants, showcasing the enormous impact small efforts can achieve.
2. **Backpacks for the Homeless**
    - In New York City, a group of friends started filling backpacks with essentials like food, toiletries, and warm clothing to distribute to homeless individuals. Their initiative has grown, helping thousands of homeless people survive the harsh winters.
3. **The Shoe That Grows**
    - Created by a small nonprofit, this innovative shoe can expand five sizes and last for years, providing children in impoverished areas with durable footwear. The impact has been significant, improving health and school attendance for countless children.

Grassroots movements and small charities show how dedicated people and communities can make a big difference. They can make a real difference by focusing on their local communities, using creative methods, and building strong connections. Planting trees, providing meals, or offering support all help hone the world into a place. Let's celebrate and support these unsung heroes, who work tirelessly to make a difference, step by step.

Chapter 11: Advocacy and Social Justice Charities

Welcome to the world of advocacy and social justice charities, where passion and purpose collide, and activism gets a charitable twist. These organizations are like superheroes in the non-profit world, with capes being a fun but suggested accessory. These charities are leading the way in fighting against racism, gender inequality, and advocating for LGBTQ+ rights. They are equipped with loud voices, legal knowledge, and a strong commitment to justice.

Advocacy and social justice charities focus on tackling the root causes of social issues, rather than offering short-term aid like other charities. It's a bit like pulling weeds—why just trim the top when you can yank out the whole darn thing? Despite scandals, these organizations strive to shape policy, raise awareness, and rally people. Who claimed saving the world is easy?

In these pages, we'll take a closer look at some of the most influential advocacy and social justice charities. We'll highlight their goals, celebrate their successes, and discuss some of the obstacles they encounter. Because in the world of social justice, transparency isn't just a buzzword—it's a necessity.

Get ready for an exciting and sometimes tiring journey into the world of advocacy and social justice charities. Prepare to be inspired, informed, and maybe even a little bit entertained. After all, who says serious work can't come with a side of humor?

Historical Context

Now that we've set the stage, let's travel back in time and explore the roots of advocacy and social justice movements. These organizations didn't just pop up overnight; they have rich histories filled with inspiring milestones and pioneering figures. By learning about the history of civil rights movements, we can better understand their significance in shaping society today.

Early Beginnings

- **Civil Rights Movement**: The origins of civil rights advocacy can be traced back to the early 20th century, with key figures like W.E.B. Du Bois and organizations such as the NAACP leading the charge against racial discrimination. In the 1950s and 1960s, the movement gained momentum. Leaders such as Martin Luther King Jr. supported peaceful protests to fight against segregation and inequality.

- **Women's Suffrage**: The fight for women's right to vote was another early and critical social justice movement. Susan B. Anthony and Elizabeth Cady Stanton fought hard for women's voting rights in the late 19th and early 20th centuries. They succeeded with the passage of the 19th Amendment in 1920.

Major Milestones

- **1960s and 1970s**: This era was marked by major social upheavals and legislative achievements in civil rights, gender equality, and environmental activism. The Civil Rights Act of 1964 and the Voting Rights Act of 1965 were landmark legislations that aimed to end racial discrimination and protect voting rights. In 1973, the feminist movement made progress with laws like Title IX and Roe v. Wade. These laws defended women's rights to education and reproductive freedom.
- **Recent Decades**: Contemporary movements have built on this legacy, adapting to new challenges and leveraging modern tools like social media. The LGBTQ+ rights movement is constantly evolving as it fights for same-sex marriage and trans rights.

Influential Figures and Organizations

- **Martin Luther King Jr.**: Known for his leadership in the Civil Rights Movement, King advocated for equality through nonviolent resistance and delivered iconic speeches like "I Have a Dream."
- **Susan B. Anthony and Elizabeth Cady Stanton**: Pioneers of the women's suffrage movement, their efforts were instrumental in securing the right to vote for women in the United States.
- **Harvey Milk**: One of the first openly gay elected officials in the

United States, Milk was a trailblazer for LGBTQ+ rights and his legacy continues to inspire activists today.

- **Organizations**: The NAACP, ACLU, and Southern Poverty Law Center have been at the forefront of civil rights advocacy for decades, each contributing significantly to the fight for justice and equality.

Understanding the history and foundations of these movements helps us grasp modern advocacy and social justice charities. These organizations, inspired by the past, continue to push for progress and challenge the status quo.

Key Characteristics of Advocacy and Social Justice Charities
Mission and Goals:

- **Addressing Inequality**: These charities focus on combating various forms of inequality, whether it's racial, gender, economic, or otherwise. Imagine them as the superheroes of the non-profit world, fighting the good fight to create a fairer society for everyone.
- **Policy Advocacy**: Instead of just helping individuals, these organizations aim to change the laws and systems that cause problems in the first place. They're the ones who knock on the doors of policymakers, ensuring that the voices of the underrepresented are heard loud and clear.
- **Community Empowerment**: Empowering communities to advocate for themselves is a cornerstone of these charities. It's like giving people the keys to their own liberation, encouraging self-sufficiency and resilience.

Activities:

- **Public Awareness Campaigns**: These organizations are masters of getting the word out. From viral social media campaigns to eye-catching billboards, they know how to capture public attention and drive home important messages.
- **Legal Support**: Providing legal aid to those who can't afford it is another crucial activity. It's like having a superhero lawyer on your

side, fighting for justice in the courtroom.

- **Grassroots Organizing**: Building movements from the ground up is essential for creating lasting change. These charities excel at mobilizing communities, organizing protests, and creating networks of activists.
- **Research and Reporting**: Gathering data and producing reports help to highlight issues and propose solutions. Think of them as the detectives of the social justice world, uncovering the facts and figures that drive their advocacy.

Black Lives Matter Global Network Foundation (BLMGNF)

Mission and Activities: The Black Lives Matter Global Network Foundation (BLMGNF) aims to eradicate white supremacy and build local power to intervene in violence inflicted on Black communities by the state and vigilantes. BLM was established in 2013 after Trayvon Martin's killer was acquitted. It has since become a global movement fighting for racial justice through protests, policy advocacy, and community organizing.

Impact and Controversies: BLM has undeniably raised significant awareness about police brutality and systemic racism. The movement was instrumental in the global protests that happened after George Floyd's murder in 2020, with millions of people joining in. Their advocacy has resulted in policy changes in multiple areas, including bans on chokeholds and the creation of civilian oversight boards for police departments.

However, the organization has faced its share of controversies. There are allegations of financial mismanagement, especially regarding the purchase of a $6 million property in Los Angeles. Critics say this was not a proper use of donated funds. BLM finished the fiscal year 2021-2022 with about $30 million in assets, showing their strong fundraising skills and the ongoing discussion about their financial transparency.

NAACP (National Association for the Advancement of Colored People)

Mission and Activities: The NAACP, established in 1909, is one of the oldest and most influential civil rights organizations in the United States. Its mission is to secure the political, educational, social, and economic equality of rights to eliminate race-based discrimination and ensure the health and well-being of all persons. The NAACP engages in litigation, advocacy, and education to achieve its goals.

Impact: The NAACP has been instrumental in numerous landmark civil rights achievements. Its legal arm, the NAACP Legal Defense and Educational Fund, played a pivotal role in the Brown v. Board of Education case, which led to the desegregation of public schools in 1954. The organization also contributed significantly to the passage of the Civil Rights Act of 1964 and the Voting Rights Act of 1965, which dismantled legal segregation and protected voting rights, respectively.

Despite its successes, the NAACP has faced criticism over the years for its perceived bureaucracy and slow response to emerging civil rights issues. Additionally, some have questioned the effectiveness of its strategies in the modern era, where new forms of activism, such as those utilized by BLM, have gained prominence. Nevertheless, the NAACP continues to be a critical player in the fight for racial equality, with a long history of significant contributions to civil rights advancements.

ACLU (American Civil Liberties Union)

Mission and Activities: The American Civil Liberties Union (ACLU) is dedicated to defending and preserving the individual rights and liberties guaranteed to every person in the United States by the Constitution and laws of the country. Founded in 1920, the ACLU works through litigation, lobbying, and public education to protect civil rights in areas such as free speech, voting rights, reproductive rights, and privacy.

Impact: The ACLU has been at the forefront of numerous landmark legal battles that have shaped American civil liberties. One of its most famous cases is **Brown v. Board of Education** (1954), which declared state laws establishing separate public schools for black and white students to be unconstitutional. The ACLU also played a crucial role in the **Roe v. Wade** decision (1973), which affirmed women's right to choose an abortion.

Lately, the ACLU has been fighting against the Trump administration's travel bans and advocating for the rights of immigrants, LGBTQ+ individuals, and prisoners. The organization has achieved success by stopping the travel ban and fighting for transgender rights in the military. Even though the ACLU has won some battles, it has been criticized for its support of free speech, particularly when it comes to defending controversial individuals and organizations. This has caused internal disagreements and public scrutiny.

Southern Poverty Law Center

Mission and Activities: The Southern Poverty Law Center (SPLC) is a nonprofit legal advocacy organization specializing in civil rights and public interest litigation. Founded in 1971, its mission is to fight hate and bigotry and to seek justice for the most vulnerable members of society. The SPLC is known for its work in tracking and exposing hate groups, litigating civil rights cases, and providing educational resources to promote tolerance.

Impact: The SPLC has made significant contributions to civil rights through its legal advocacy and educational efforts. The Intelligence Project monitors hate groups and extremists in the U.S. It provides valuable information on domestic terrorism and hate crimes to law enforcement and the public. The SPLC has successfully sued the Ku Klux Klan, causing them financial damage and forcing the closure of many Klan chapters.

The SPLC also founded **Teaching Tolerance** (now known as Learning for Justice), an educational program aimed at promoting diversity and inclusion in schools. Despite these achievements, the SPLC has not been without controversy. The organization had problems internally in recent years, with allegations of discrimination and misconduct. This led to the co-founder Morris Dees resigning. Some critics say that the SPLC defines hate groups too broadly and for political reasons.

Amnesty International

Mission and Activities: Amnesty International is a global movement of more than 10 million people who campaign for a world where human rights are enjoyed by all. Amnesty International, founded in 1961, works to stop human rights abuses and seek justice for victims. The organization is neutral and independent, making sure its actions are not influenced by the government, politics, or corporations.

Impact: Amnesty International has been instrumental in numerous global human rights victories. One of its biggest achievements is the successful campaign against the death penalty, leading to its abolition in several countries. Amnesty's efforts have helped free thousands of innocent people who were imprisoned for their beliefs.

Amnesty's reports and advocacy have led to policy changes globally, helping create international human rights standards. Its campaigns have convinced governments to sign treaties against torture and unlawful detention. Amnesty has been criticized for bias in its reporting and for being selective in its criticism of governments. Additionally, internal challenges, such as accusations of workplace harassment, have sometimes overshadowed its mission.

Human Rights Campaign (HRC)

Mission and Activities: The Human Rights Campaign (HRC) is the largest LGBTQ+ advocacy group and political lobbying organization in the United States. Founded in 1980, HRC's mission is to ensure that LGBTQ+ people are treated as full and equal citizens across the country and around the world. The organization does various activities, such as advocating for equality laws, raising awareness, and supporting LGBTQ+ friendly politicians.

Impact: HRC has played a pivotal role in some of the most significant advances for LGBTQ+ rights in recent history. The organization played a big role in the fight for marriage equality, which led to the Supreme Court legalizing same-sex marriage across the country. HRC supports laws that protect LGBTQ+ individuals from discrimination in employment, housing, and public accommodations.

The HRC Foundation runs several initiatives aimed at improving the lives of LGBTQ+ people, including programs focused on healthcare, workplace equality, and the needs of LGBTQ+ youth. However, the HRC has faced criticism for its internal practices and leadership decisions, with some advocates arguing that it does not adequately represent the diversity within the LGBTQ+ community, particularly regarding racial and gender inclusivity. These criticisms highlight the ongoing challenges within advocacy organizations to balance broad representation with effective leadership.

Planned Parenthood

Mission and Activities: Planned Parenthood is dedicated to providing comprehensive reproductive health care services, education, and advocacy. Founded in 1916 by Margaret Sanger, it offers a wide range of services including contraception, STI testing and treatment, cancer screenings, and safe and legal abortions. The organization also works tirelessly to advocate for policies that protect and expand reproductive rights, ensuring that everyone has access to the care they need.

Impact: Planned Parenthood serves millions of people each year, many of whom rely on their services as a primary source of healthcare. They have been a key player in significant legal battles to protect reproductive rights, such as the landmark case Roe v. Wade. However, the organization has faced its share of controversy, especially from anti-abortion groups. Funding for Planned Parenthood has been a hot-button issue in U.S. politics, with debates often centered around their abortion services despite the fact that these account for a small percentage of their overall operations. Their commitment to comprehensive reproductive health and rights continues to make a significant impact on public health and personal autonomy.

Environmental Defense Fund (EDF)

Mission and Activities: The Environmental Defense Fund (EDF) is a leading environmental advocacy group founded in 1967. Its goal is to protect the environment by addressing climate change, pollution, and sustainable agriculture. EDF uses a combination of science, economics, law, and innovative private-sector partnerships to create solutions that benefit both people and the environment.

Impact: EDF has achieved numerous environmental victories, including playing a pivotal role in the creation of the U.S. Clean Air Act and the ban on DDT. They have been instrumental in the fight against climate change, advocating for carbon pricing and clean energy policies. EDF also works on corporate partnerships to promote sustainable business practices. Despite these successes, the organization has faced criticism for working too closely with businesses and sometimes compromising on environmental principles. Nonetheless, EDF's innovative and collaborative approach has led to substantial progress in environmental protection and policy.

Equal Justice Initiative (EJI)

Mission and Activities: Founded in 1989 by Bryan Stevenson, the Equal Justice Initiative (EJI) aims to end mass incarceration and excessive punishment in the United States, challenge racial and economic injustice, and protect basic human rights for the most vulnerable people in American society. EJI provides legal representation to prisoners who may have been wrongly convicted, unfairly sentenced, or abused in state jails and prisons.

Impact: EJI has successfully overturned numerous wrongful convictions and death sentences, highlighting systemic flaws in the U.S. justice system. Their work on behalf of juvenile offenders led to landmark Supreme Court rulings that declared mandatory life-without-parole sentences for children unconstitutional. EJI also created the National Memorial for Peace and Justice, which commemorates the victims of lynching in the U.S. While widely praised for its impactful work, EJI operates in a contentious area of social justice, often facing pushback from those resistant to criminal justice reform. Their commitment to addressing and remedying racial injustice and mass incarceration continues to drive significant legal and cultural change.

Chapter 12: Volunteering - Time as a Valuable Resource

Enter the world of volunteering, where your time becomes a precious gift that makes a difference. This chapter will discuss why volunteering is important, the different opportunities available, and how it benefits communities and volunteers. We'll share fun facts about famous volunteers and interesting statistics and stories about volunteering.

Importance of Volunteering

Volunteering is an invaluable act of service where individuals offer their time and skills without financial compensation. Here's why volunteering is just as important as monetary donations:

1. Filling Critical Gaps

Volunteers often provide essential services that organizations might not be able to afford otherwise. From tutoring children to assisting in disaster relief, volunteers help fill critical gaps and support community needs.

2. Building Stronger Communities

Volunteering fosters a sense of community and solidarity. It brings people together, creating a network of support and collaboration that strengthens the social fabric.

3. Skill Development

For volunteers, the experience can be a powerful tool for personal and professional growth. Volunteering offers opportunities to develop new skills, gain experience, and enhance employability.

4. Creating Positive Change

By donating their time, volunteers can drive significant social change. Whether it's advocating for policy changes, protecting the environment, or supporting vulnerable populations, volunteers are often at the forefront of positive societal shifts.

Types of Volunteering Opportunities

Volunteering opportunities are diverse and cater to various interests, skills, and availability. Here are some different ways to get involved:

1. Local Volunteering

- **Community Centers:** Volunteers can assist with after-school programs, senior services, and community events.
- **Food Banks and Shelters:** Helping to prepare and distribute meals or organize donations.
- **Environmental Cleanups:** Participating in local cleanups to maintain parks, beaches, and public spaces.

2. National Volunteering

- **Disaster Relief:** Organizations like the Red Cross mobilize volunteers to support relief efforts during natural disasters.
- **Healthcare Services:** Volunteers can help at hospitals, clinics, or blood donation drives.
- **Educational Programs:** Mentoring, tutoring, or supporting literacy programs across the country.

3. International Volunteering

- **Global NGOs:** Volunteering with organizations like Doctors Without Borders or Habitat for Humanity to support international development and humanitarian efforts.
- **Conservation Projects:** Joining international projects focused on wildlife conservation, reforestation, or marine protection.
- **Cultural Exchange Programs:** Participating in programs that promote cultural exchange and mutual understanding.

Impact of Volunteering

Volunteering creates a ripple effect of positive impacts that extend beyond the immediate act of service. Here's how it benefits both communities and volunteers:

1. Community Benefits

- **Enhanced Services:** Volunteers help provide critical services that improve the quality of life for community members.
- **Economic Impact:** Volunteering can contribute to economic

stability by supporting local organizations and reducing costs for essential services.

- **Social Cohesion:** Volunteering promotes social cohesion by bringing diverse groups together and fostering a sense of belonging.

2. Volunteer Benefits

- **Mental Health:** Volunteering is linked to lower rates of depression and increased life satisfaction due to the sense of purpose and connection it provides.
- **Physical Health:** Engaging in physical activities through volunteering can improve overall health and well-being.
- **Networking:** Volunteering offers opportunities to meet new people, build professional networks, and establish meaningful relationships.

Useless Helpful Tidbits

1. **Mother Teresa:** Before founding the Missionaries of Charity, Mother Teresa volunteered as a teacher in Calcutta, India.
2. **Princess Diana:** Known as the "People's Princess," Diana volunteered extensively, focusing on causes such as homelessness, leprosy, and HIV/AIDS awareness.
3. **Bill Gates:** In addition to his philanthropic efforts, Bill Gates volunteers his time for educational and global health initiatives through the Bill & Melinda Gates Foundation.

Statistics on Volunteerism

1. **Global Participation:** According to the United Nations, approximately 1 billion people around the world volunteer annually.
2. **Volunteer Demographics:** In the U.S., about 25% of adults volunteer, contributing an estimated 8 billion hours of service each year.
3. **Economic Value:** The economic value of volunteer work in the U.S. is estimated to be around $167 billion annually.

Quirky Volunteering Experiences

1. **Penguin Patrol:** In New Zealand, volunteers participate in "penguin patrols" to help little blue penguins cross busy roads safely.
2. **Dog Cuddling:** Some animal shelters offer "dog cuddling" programs where volunteers spend time cuddling and socializing with dogs to improve their chances of adoption.
3. **Laughter Yoga:** Volunteers in India lead laughter yoga sessions in parks, combining voluntary laughter exercises with yoga breathing techniques to promote wellness and social connection.

Volunteering is a powerful way to contribute to the greater good, offering valuable benefits to both communities and individuals. Whether it's helping out at a local shelter, participating in international conservation efforts, or engaging in unique and quirky volunteer experiences, donating time can create lasting positive impacts. So, roll up your sleeves and get involved—your time is one of the most precious gifts you can give.

Chapter 13: Disaster Relief and Emergency Aid

In this chapter, we delve into the critical realm of disaster relief and emergency aid, exploring how charities and organizations respond to crises, profiling key players in disaster relief, and examining the challenges and successes in this field. We'll also uncover interesting facts, share statistics, and highlight some quirky stories from the field.

Overview of Disaster Relief Efforts

Disaster relief efforts are essential responses to natural or human-made disasters, aiming to provide immediate assistance to those affected. These efforts include:

1. Immediate Response

- **Search and Rescue:** Teams are deployed to locate and save individuals trapped or endangered by the disaster.
- **Emergency Medical Care:** Medical personnel provide urgent care to the injured, often setting up field hospitals and mobile clinics.

2. Provision of Basic Needs

- **Shelter:** Temporary shelters are established to house displaced individuals and families.
- **Food and Water:** Distribution of food and clean water to prevent malnutrition and dehydration.
- **Clothing and Hygiene:** Supplying essential clothing and hygiene products to maintain health and dignity.

3. Recovery and Rehabilitation

- **Infrastructure Repair:** Rebuilding homes, schools, and essential infrastructure.
- **Mental Health Support:** Providing counseling and psychological support to help individuals cope with trauma.

- **Community Rebuilding:** Long-term support to restore economic stability and community resilience.

Key Organizations in Disaster Relief
Red Cross
Overview: The Red Cross is one of the most recognized disaster relief organizations globally, providing emergency assistance, disaster preparedness education, and recovery support. **Notable Efforts:** The Red Cross has been instrumental in responding to major disasters such as Hurricane Katrina, the 2010 Haiti earthquake, and the COVID-19 pandemic. **Challenges:** Balancing the immediate need for aid with long-term recovery efforts, and managing large-scale logistics.

Médecins Sans Frontières (Doctors Without Borders)
Overview: Médecins Sans Frontières (MSF) is an international medical humanitarian organization that provides emergency medical care in conflict zones and areas affected by disease outbreaks. **Notable Efforts:** MSF's response to the Ebola outbreak in West Africa, providing medical care in war-torn regions like Syria, and addressing malnutrition crises in Africa. **Challenges:** Operating in high-risk environments, ensuring the safety of staff, and managing limited resources.

Federal Emergency Management Agency (FEMA)
Overview: FEMA is a U.S. government agency that coordinates the federal response to disasters, providing financial assistance, logistical support, and recovery programs. **Notable Efforts:** FEMA's response to natural disasters such as hurricanes, wildfires, and floods, as well as its role in the aftermath of the September 11 attacks. **Challenges:** Coordinating efforts across multiple levels of government, dealing with bureaucratic delays, and managing public expectations.

Challenges and Successes
Common Challenges

1. **Logistical Coordination**
   - Efficiently distributing aid in disaster zones, often hindered by damaged infrastructure and limited access.
2. **Resource Allocation**

- Ensuring adequate resources and personnel are available, often in the face of overwhelming demand and limited supplies.

3. **Cultural Sensitivity**
   - Providing aid that respects local customs and practices, and effectively communicating with diverse populations.

4. **Funding and Sustainability**
   - Securing sufficient funding for immediate response and long-term recovery, while maintaining donor interest and support.

Successful Aid Efforts

1. **2010 Haiti Earthquake**
   - The international community's rapid response, including the Red Cross and MSF, provided critical medical care, shelter, and food to millions of affected individuals. The efforts helped prevent large-scale outbreaks of diseases and initiated rebuilding efforts.

2. **Ebola Outbreak in West Africa**
   - MSF's deployment of medical personnel and establishment of treatment centers played a pivotal role in controlling the outbreak. Their efforts, combined with international support, eventually brought the epidemic under control.

3. **Hurricane Harvey (2017)**
   - FEMA's coordination with state and local agencies, along with the support of numerous NGOs, facilitated efficient rescue operations, provision of basic needs, and significant recovery assistance, helping communities rebuild.

Useless Helpful Tidbits

1. **Global Reach:** The Red Cross has a presence in nearly every country in the world, allowing for swift and coordinated disaster response.
2. **First Responders:** Local communities are often the first responders

to disasters, providing immediate aid and support before international help arrives.

Statistics on Disaster Response

1. **Financial Impact:** In 2020, global economic losses from natural disasters were estimated at $210 billion.
2. **Human Impact:** Natural disasters affected over 98 million people worldwide in 2019, with thousands of lives lost and millions displaced.

Quirky Stories from the Field

1. **Animal Rescues:** During Hurricane Katrina, rescue teams not only saved humans but also thousands of pets, reuniting many with their owners and establishing animal shelters for displaced pets.
2. **Floating Libraries:** In the aftermath of floods in Pakistan, volunteers set up "floating libraries" on boats to provide books and educational materials to children stranded by floodwaters.

Disaster relief and emergency aid are crucial components of humanitarian efforts, providing lifesaving support and helping communities recover and rebuild. Despite the challenges, the dedication and resilience of disaster relief organizations and volunteers ensure that help reaches those in need. Whether through medical care, shelter, or innovative solutions like floating libraries, these efforts highlight the remarkable capacity of humanity to come together in times of crisis.

Chapter 14: Innovative Fundraising Techniques

Welcome to the cutting-edge world of fundraising, where creativity and technology merge to fuel charitable giving. In this chapter, we'll explore modern fundraising methods, examine how technology is revolutionizing the field, and highlight successful campaigns that have set new standards. As always, we'll add a sprinkle of fun facts, insightful statistics, and quirky fundraising stories.

Modern Fundraising Methods

Charities are constantly evolving their strategies to attract donors and sustain their missions. Here are some of the most innovative fundraising methods making waves today:

1. Crowdfunding

Crowdfunding platforms like GoFundMe, Kickstarter, and Indiegogo enable charities to raise small amounts of money from a large number of people, leveraging social networks to reach potential donors globally.

2. Peer-to-Peer Fundraising

This method empowers supporters to create their own fundraising campaigns on behalf of a charity. Participants often use personal stories and social media to engage their networks, multiplying the reach and impact.

3. Virtual Events

With the rise of digital platforms, virtual fundraising events like webinars, online auctions, and virtual runs or walks have become popular. These events allow charities to engage with supporters remotely, reducing costs and expanding their reach.

4. Recurring Giving Programs

Monthly giving programs provide a steady and predictable source of income for charities. Donors commit to regular contributions, often in exchange for exclusive updates or perks, fostering a deeper connection to the cause.

5. Corporate Partnerships and Sponsorships

Charities collaborate with businesses to raise funds through cause-marketing campaigns, employee giving programs, and event sponsorships. These partnerships benefit both parties by enhancing corporate social responsibility (CSR) and providing charities with financial support.

Impact of Technology on Fundraising

Technology has transformed fundraising, making it easier, faster, and more efficient. Here's how:

1. Online Donation Platforms

Websites and mobile apps facilitate easy and secure online donations, allowing supporters to contribute from anywhere at any time. Platforms like PayPal, Stripe, and GiveDirectly streamline the donation process.

2. Social Media

Social media platforms like Facebook, Instagram, and Twitter are powerful tools for raising awareness and funds. Charities use these platforms to share compelling stories, run fundraising campaigns, and engage with supporters in real-time.

3. Artificial Intelligence (AI)

AI helps charities analyze donor data, personalize communication, and predict giving behaviors. This enables more effective targeting and engagement strategies, increasing donor retention and contributions.

4. Blockchain and Cryptocurrencies

Blockchain technology ensures transparency and security in transactions, building trust among donors. Accepting cryptocurrencies like Bitcoin allows charities to tap into a new donor base and offers a modern, tech-savvy way to give.

5. Virtual Reality (VR) and Augmented Reality (AR)

VR and AR create immersive experiences that can engage donors on a deeper level. For example, VR can transport donors to the field, allowing them to see firsthand the impact of their contributions.

Successful Fundraising Campaigns

1. ALS Ice Bucket Challenge

In 2014, the ALS Ice Bucket Challenge went viral, raising over $115 million for ALS research. Participants shared videos of themselves being doused with ice water and challenged others to do the same, creating a global movement.

2. Charity: Water's Birthday Campaign

CHARITY GIVING DONATION REVELATION

Charity: Water encourages supporters to pledge their birthdays, asking for donations instead of gifts. This simple yet powerful idea has raised millions, funding clean water projects around the world.

3. Movember

The Movember Foundation challenges men to grow mustaches during November to raise awareness and funds for men's health issues like prostate cancer and mental health. The campaign combines fun and fundraising, generating widespread participation and support.

Useless Helpful Tidbits

1. **First Crowdfunding Campaign:** The Statue of Liberty's pedestal was funded by a crowdfunding campaign in 1885, raising over $100,000 (equivalent to about $2.5 million today) from more than 160,000 donors.
2. **Longest Charity Run:** In 2013, Rob Young set the record for the longest charity run by covering 10,000 miles across the UK in 420 days, raising funds for various children's charities.

Statistics on the Effectiveness of Different Fundraising Methods

1. **Online Giving Growth:** Online giving grew by 21% in 2020, with digital donations accounting for 13% of all charitable giving in the U.S.
2. **Impact of Recurring Donations:** Donors who set up recurring donations give 42% more annually than one-time donors.

Quirky Fundraising Campaigns

1. **Pajama Walks:** Some charities organize "pajama walks" where participants wear pajamas and stroll through their communities to raise funds and awareness. This fun and cozy event attracts families and friends, creating a relaxed fundraising atmosphere.
2. **Beard-A-Thon:** During hockey season, fans and players grow beards and raise money for charitable causes. Participants get sponsors for their beards, with all proceeds going to the chosen charity.

3. **Goat Yoga Fundraisers:** Combining yoga with the playful presence of goats, these unique fundraising events have gained popularity. Participants pay to join yoga sessions with goats, with proceeds supporting local animal shelters and farms.

Innovative fundraising techniques are crucial for charities to stay relevant and effective in today's digital world. By leveraging technology, creativity, and the power of social networks, charities can reach new heights in their fundraising efforts. Whether through viral campaigns, virtual events, or quirky initiatives, the possibilities are endless. So, let's embrace these innovations and continue to support the causes we care about in exciting and impactful ways.

Chapter 15: Philanthropy and the Wealthy

In this chapter, we delve into the significant role that wealthy individuals play in charitable giving. We'll profile some of the most notable philanthropists, explore the impact of their large donations, and share interesting facts, statistics, and quirky stories about these generous benefactors.

Role of the Wealthy in Charitable Giving

Affluent individuals have a profound impact on charitable giving, leveraging their wealth to support a wide range of causes. Here's how they contribute:

1. Substantial Financial Contributions

Wealthy donors often make large donations that can significantly advance the missions of charities. These contributions can fund major projects, support research, and create lasting change.

2. Establishing Foundations

Many affluent individuals establish their own foundations to focus on specific issues. These foundations can operate on a large scale, addressing complex problems with strategic, long-term approaches.

3. Influence and Advocacy

Wealthy philanthropists often use their influence to advocate for causes they care about, raising awareness and inspiring others to contribute. Their involvement can attract media attention and public interest, amplifying the impact of their efforts.

4. Innovative Approaches

With substantial resources at their disposal, wealthy donors can support innovative approaches to solving social problems. They often fund pilot programs and new technologies that can lead to groundbreaking solutions.

Famous Philanthropists

1. Bill Gates

Contributions: Through the Bill & Melinda Gates Foundation, Gates has donated billions to global health, education, and poverty alleviation. The foundation has been instrumental in efforts to eradicate diseases like polio and malaria. **Impact:** Gates' philanthropy has transformed global health and education, improving millions of lives worldwide.

2. Warren Buffett

Contributions: Buffett has pledged to give away 99% of his wealth, primarily through the Gates Foundation. His annual donations have funded various initiatives in health, education, and poverty reduction. **Impact:** Buffett's significant contributions have amplified the work of many charitable organizations, driving large-scale social change.

3. MacKenzie Scott

Contributions: Since her divorce from Jeff Bezos, Scott has donated billions to various causes, including racial equality, LGBTQ+ rights, and public health. Her approach emphasizes speed and flexibility, often making large, unrestricted grants. **Impact:** Scott's philanthropy has provided immediate and substantial support to underfunded organizations, making a direct and swift impact on numerous communities.

4. Michael Bloomberg

Contributions: Bloomberg has given billions through his foundation, Bloomberg Philanthropies, focusing on public health, education, the environment, and the arts. He is also a major supporter of climate change initiatives. **Impact:** Bloomberg's donations have supported a wide array of projects, from reducing tobacco use worldwide to improving urban infrastructure and combatting climate change.

Impact of Large Donations

Large donations from wealthy individuals can transform the landscape of charitable giving in several ways:

1. Enabling Major Projects

Significant contributions allow charities to undertake large-scale projects that require substantial funding. This can include building hospitals, funding extensive research, or launching nationwide educational programs.

2. Sustainable Funding

Large donations can provide sustainable funding for charities, allowing them to plan long-term projects and initiatives without the constant pressure of fundraising.

3. Leveraging Additional Support

High-profile donations often inspire others to give, leveraging additional support and multiplying the impact of the initial contribution.

4. Driving Innovation

Wealthy donors can fund innovative solutions and new technologies, driving progress in various fields and creating models that can be replicated elsewhere.

Useless Helpful Tidbits

1. **Andrew Carnegie:** A pioneer of modern philanthropy, Carnegie donated over $350 million (equivalent to billions today) to libraries, education, and peace initiatives. His philosophy of "giving while living" has inspired many current philanthropists.
2. **John D. Rockefeller:** Rockefeller's philanthropic efforts established institutions like the University of Chicago and the Rockefeller Foundation, which has contributed significantly to public health, medical research, and the arts.

Statistics on Large Donations

1. **Top Donors:** In 2020, the top 50 U.S. donors contributed a combined total of $24.7 billion to charitable causes.
2. **Influence of the Wealthy:** The top 1% of donors account for more than a third of all charitable donations in the U.S., highlighting the significant influence of wealthy individuals on the nonprofit sector.

Quirky Stories About Wealthy Donors

1. **Anonymous Giver:** Chuck Feeney, co-founder of Duty-Free Shoppers, quietly gave away his entire fortune of over $8 billion, living a life of frugality while supporting causes worldwide. His stealth philanthropy earned him the nickname "The James Bond of Philanthropy."
2. **Power of the Beard:** Billionaire Richard Branson once shaved his iconic beard after raising over $1 million for a children's charity. This quirky fundraising effort drew attention and substantial donations.

Philanthropy by the wealthy plays a crucial role in addressing global challenges and supporting charitable causes. Through substantial financial contributions, the establishment of foundations, and the leveraging of their influence, affluent individuals can drive significant and lasting change. Whether through strategic donations, innovative initiatives, or quirky fundraising campaigns, the impact of their generosity is felt far and wide, proving that with great wealth comes great responsibility—and tremendous potential for good.

Chapter 16: Ethical Considerations in Charitable Giving

Welcome to the chapter where we delve into the moral compass guiding charitable giving. Ethical considerations are paramount to ensuring that donations make a positive impact without inadvertently causing harm. We'll explore the importance of transparency and accountability, provide guidance on avoiding unethical charities, and share some intriguing tidbits about ethical giving.

Ethics in Charitable Giving

Ethical charitable giving involves ensuring that donations are used effectively and responsibly. Here are some key ethical considerations for donors:

1. Intent and Impact

- **Intent:** Donors should reflect on their motivations for giving. Are they driven by a genuine desire to help, or are there other incentives like tax breaks or social recognition?
- **Impact:** Consider the long-term impact of donations. Effective giving should lead to sustainable, positive changes rather than temporary fixes.

2. Respect for Beneficiaries

- **Dignity and Privacy:** Charities should respect the dignity and privacy of their beneficiaries. This includes how they use images and stories of those they help.
- **Community Involvement:** Beneficiaries should be involved in decision-making processes to ensure that aid meets their actual needs and respects local customs and traditions.

3. Avoiding Harm

- **Unintended Consequences:** Be aware of how aid can sometimes cause harm, such as creating dependency, undermining local businesses, or perpetuating inequalities.

- **Conflict Sensitivity:** In conflict zones, aid should be distributed in ways that do not exacerbate tensions or contribute to violence.

Transparency and Accountability

Transparency and accountability are crucial for building trust and ensuring that donations are used effectively. Here's why they matter:

1. Financial Transparency

- **Clear Reporting:** Charities should provide clear, accessible reports on how funds are used, including detailed financial statements and breakdowns of administrative costs versus program spending.
- **Independent Audits:** Regular independent audits can help ensure that charities are managing their funds responsibly.

2. Program Accountability

- **Impact Measurement:** Charities should track and report on the outcomes of their programs, showing donors the tangible impact of their contributions.
- **Feedback Mechanisms:** Implementing feedback mechanisms allows beneficiaries and donors to voice concerns and suggestions, fostering continuous improvement.

3. Governance and Ethics Policies

- **Board Oversight:** A well-functioning board of directors can provide oversight and strategic direction, ensuring that the charity adheres to its mission and values.
- **Ethics Policies:** Charities should have clear ethics policies, including codes of conduct for staff and volunteers, to prevent abuse and misconduct.

Avoiding Unethical Charities

CHARITY GIVING DONATION REVELATION

Identifying and avoiding unethical charities is critical to ensuring that donations are not misused. Here are some tips:

1. Research and Vetting

- **Charity Watchdogs:** Use resources like Charity Navigator, GuideStar, and the BBB Wise Giving Alliance to research charities' financial health, transparency, and accountability.
- **Read Reviews:** Look for reviews from other donors and beneficiaries to get a sense of the charity's reputation and effectiveness.

2. Red Flags to Watch For

- **Lack of Transparency:** Be wary of charities that do not provide clear financial reports or detailed information about their programs.
- **High Administrative Costs:** Excessive spending on administration and fundraising, with little going to actual programs, is a warning sign.
- **Aggressive Fundraising Tactics:** Pressure to donate immediately or share personal financial information can indicate unethical practices.

3. Ask Questions

- **Specific Impact:** Ask how donations will be used and what specific impact they will have.
- **Governance:** Inquire about the charity's governance structure and ethics policies.

Useless Helpful Tidbits

1. **Effective Altruism:** This movement advocates using evidence and reason to determine the most effective ways to benefit others. It encourages donors to focus on causes that can have the greatest impact per dollar spent.
2. **GiveWell:** An organization that conducts in-depth research to identify the most effective charities, helping donors make informed

decisions.

Stories of Charity Scandals

1. **The Wounded Warrior Project:** In 2016, the Wounded Warrior Project faced scrutiny over allegations of excessive spending on administrative costs and lavish events. Following the scandal, the organization made significant changes to its leadership and financial practices to regain trust.
2. **Cancer Fund of America:** This organization, along with several affiliates, was shut down in 2015 after it was revealed that only a small fraction of donations went to actual cancer patients, with most funds used for personal expenses and salaries.

Tips for Ethical Donating

1. **Do Your Homework:** Thoroughly research charities before donating to ensure they are reputable and effective.
2. **Give Directly:** Consider giving directly to beneficiaries or through platforms that facilitate direct cash transfers, allowing recipients to decide how best to use the funds.
3. **Support Transparency:** Choose charities that are transparent about their operations and impact, and encourage others to do the same.

Ethical considerations in charitable giving ensure that donations lead to positive, sustainable outcomes. By prioritizing transparency, accountability, and a deep respect for beneficiaries, donors can help create a more effective and just charitable sector. Remember to do your research, ask the right questions, and support organizations that align with these ethical principles, making each donation count towards meaningful change.

Chapter 17: Top 10 Charity Scandals and Misrepresentations

Welcome to the abyss where we uncover the truth behind popular charities. While our book is generally a light-hearted romp through the world of philanthropy, this chapter dives into the serious business of accountability. When you donate money, you should know if it's going towards important research or luxury trips for someone.

We've all seen the tear-jerking ads and the uplifting success stories, but behind the scenes, it's not always rainbows and miracles. Even well-known charities can have hidden problems, like misusing money or spending too much on administrative costs. So buckle up, dear reader, as we count down the top ten most scandalous and misrepresented charities. You might laugh, you might cry, but most importantly, you'll be informed.

#10. Shriners Hospitals for Children

Let's start our countdown with Shriners Hospitals for Children, an organization known for its extensive network of hospitals that provide specialized care for children at no cost to their families. Sounds fantastic, right? And it is—up to a point.

Shriners Hospitals for Children is supported by a substantial endowment, reported to be around $8.2 billion as of 2012. This endowment ensures the hospitals can keep running, even if fundraising doesn't meet expectations. However, having extra funds means that a large part of the money raised from their commercials doesn't go directly to helping patients. In fact, some of it funds the lavish lifestyles of the board members, complete with first-class flights and temporary housing allowances.

Approximately 80% of the funds raised by Shriners are dedicated to patient care, research, and education, which is commendable. But the remaining 20%—well, let's just say it's not always spent on Band-Aids and lollipops. Critics have pointed out the high compensation-related expenses and other perks enjoyed by the top brass. So while those TV ads might tug at your heartstrings, it's worth remembering that not every penny is going to the kids.

#9. Susan G. Komen for the Cure

Susan G. Komen for the Cure, one of the most recognizable breast cancer charities, has been both a pioneer and a controversial figure in the nonprofit world. Founded in 1982, the organization has raised billions for breast cancer research, education, and support programs. The pink ribbons and Race for the Cure have raised a lot of money and awareness for breast cancer. However, behind the pink ribbons and marathon walks, there have been several bumps on the road.

Positive Impact

Komen has undeniably contributed to the fight against breast cancer. The organization has funded groundbreaking research, supported education and screening programs, and provided crucial support to breast cancer patients and their families. Their advocacy efforts have also led to increased public awareness and early detection, which have been instrumental in improving breast cancer survival rates. And let's face it, they've managed to make it socially acceptable to talk about boobs in public for a good cause—a feat in itself!

Criticisms and Challenges

- **Funding Controversies**: The charity faced a major backlash in 2012 when it decided to stop funding Planned Parenthood's breast cancer screening programs. This move, perceived as politically motivated, caused an uproar among supporters and led to a significant drop in donations. Komen eventually reversed its decision, but the damage was done, and trust was eroded faster than you can say "pink ribbon."

- **Fund Allocation**: Additionally, Komen has been criticized for how it allocates its funds. A substantial portion of the donations goes towards marketing, administrative costs, and salaries. Critics argue that money should be spent on cancer research and supporting patients instead of on brand promotion and extravagant events. Some of the funds raised for breast cancer programs are used for operational expenses instead. So while you're out there racing for a cure, a good chunk of your donation might be racing towards a marketing budget.

Despite the controversies, Susan G. Komen for the Cure has made undeniable contributions to the fight against breast cancer. They have funded important research and supported countless women globally. However, it serves as a reminder of the importance of transparency and accountability in the nonprofit sector.

#8. PETA (People for the Ethical Treatment of Animals)

PETA is famous for its powerful campaigns against animal cruelty, sometimes using provocative tactics to raise awareness. The organization has raised awareness about animal rights, but it has faced criticism for euthanizing many animals at its shelters. PETA has been accused of hypocrisy for euthanizing many of the animals it receives, despite advocating for animal rights.

Positive Impact

PETA has achieved significant victories in the fight for animal rights, influencing legislation and changing corporate practices. Their campaigns have convinced companies to be more humane, like stopping animal testing and improving farm animal conditions. PETA's efforts have undoubtedly raised public awareness about animal cruelty and prompted many to adopt more ethical lifestyles. Their "I'd rather go naked than wear fur" campaign, for instance, has become iconic (and not just because it involves a lot of nudity).

Financial Efficiency and Allocation

PETA is often criticized for how it allocates its funds. In 2021, PETA reported revenue of approximately $66 million, with 83% spent on programs to help animals, 15% on fundraising, and 2% on management and general expenses. Critics argue that the money spent on provocative advertising campaigns, such as celebrity endorsements and public stunts, could be better utilized directly aiding animals.

Euthanasia Rates

Despite its advocacy for animal rights, PETA has been criticized for the high number of animals it euthanizes each year. In 2021, PETA euthanized about 65% of the animals it took in at its shelter in Norfolk, Virginia. Critics argue that this contradicts the organization's mission and point to alternatives that could be employed to save more animals. PETA defends its practices by stating that many of the animals they take in are sick, injured, or otherwise unadoptable. It's a bit like saying "We love animals... just not these ones."

Campaign Highlights

PETA's campaigns have ranged from the ingenious to the outrageous. Their "I'd rather go naked than wear fur" campaign has featured celebrities from all walks of life stripping down for the cause. They have also targeted companies like McDonald's and KFC, pushing for better treatment of animals in the food industry. PETA's ability to generate media attention is unparalleled, often leveraging shock value to bring attention to animal rights issues.

Controversial Tactics

PETA's use of controversial tactics has sparked debates about the ethics and effectiveness of their methods. They have been known to employ graphic imagery and sensationalist messages to get their point across. For example, they once compared the suffering of animals to the Holocaust, a move that was widely condemned and seen as highly insensitive. While these tactics have kept animal welfare issues in the public eye, they have also alienated potential supporters and provoked backlash.

Financial Controversies

PETA's financial management has also been scrutinized. In 2021, the organization spent $9.5 million on fundraising, a figure some donors find excessive given the organization's overall revenue. Additionally, PETA's focus on high-profile advertising campaigns raises questions about the balance between raising awareness and directly supporting animal welfare initiatives.

Trivia and Fun Facts

- **Iconic Campaigns**: The "I'd rather go naked than wear fur" campaign has featured celebrities like Pamela Anderson and Eva Mendes.
- **Celebrity Endorsements**: PETA has garnered support from numerous celebrities, including Sir Paul McCartney and Alec Baldwin.
- **Creative Protests**: PETA once offered to pay the city of Detroit's water bills for residents if they agreed to go vegan for a month.
- **Naked Ambition**: PETA staff have been known to strip down to protest fur, sometimes in freezing weather. Dedication or madness? You decide.

Despite these controversies, PETA's impact on animal rights cannot be denied. Their controversial methods, while divisive, have kept animal welfare issues in the public eye and led to significant changes in corporate and legislative practices. In other words, they know how to make a splash—even if it sometimes means getting a little wet in the process.

#7. Salvation Army

The Salvation Army is renowned for its widespread charitable work, particularly during the holiday season with its iconic red kettles and bell ringers. However, the organization has faced numerous allegations of discrimination, particularly against the LGBTQ+ community. Critics argue that these discriminatory practices undermine the inclusive mission the charity claims to uphold.

Positive Impact

The Salvation Army provides a wide range of social services, including disaster relief, rehabilitation programs, and assistance to the homeless. Operating in over 130 countries, it makes a significant impact on millions of lives through its various programs. Whether it's providing shelter, food, or a friendly face, The Salvation Army often acts as a lifeline for those in dire straits. Their ability to mobilize volunteers and resources quickly in times of need is one of their strongest assets.

- **Disaster Relief**: During Hurricane Katrina, The Salvation Army provided over 5.7 million meals, 8.3 million drinks, and 7.5 million snacks to survivors and rescue workers.
- **Homeless Services**: Each year, they provide more than 10 million nights of lodging to homeless individuals.
- **Rehabilitation Programs**: Their Adult Rehabilitation Centers help over 150,000 people annually to overcome addiction and regain their independence.

Financial Efficiency and Allocation

In 2021, The Salvation Army reported revenue of approximately $3.6 billion. They spend about 82% of their budget on program services, with the remaining 18% allocated to administrative and fundraising expenses. This allocation allows them to maintain a broad array of services while ensuring a significant portion of donations directly aids those in need.

- **Fundraising**: The iconic red kettles seen during the holiday season raised around $126 million in 2021 alone. This grassroots fundraising effort is crucial for funding their extensive services.
- **Program Services**: A significant portion of their budget supports emergency shelter, food pantries, and disaster relief efforts, ensuring that donations have a direct impact on those in need.

Criticisms and Challenges

While The Salvation Army is praised for its comprehensive approach to social services, it has faced criticism, particularly regarding allegations of discrimination against LGBTQ+ individuals. These controversies have raised questions about the organization's commitment to inclusivity and equality.

- **Discrimination Allegations**: The organization has been accused of discriminating against LGBTQ+ individuals in both their employment practices and the services they provide. These allegations have led to calls for greater inclusivity and transparency within the organization. Efforts have been made to address these concerns, but the accusations have undoubtedly tarnished its reputation.
- **Fund Allocation**: Concerns have also been raised about how funds are allocated within the organization. While The Salvation Army does provide extensive services, questions have been raised about the proportion of funds spent on administrative and promotional activities versus direct aid. Critics argue that more transparency is needed to ensure that donations are used effectively and ethically.

Trivia and Fun Facts

- **Iconic Red Kettles**: The red kettles date back to 1891, when Captain Joseph McFee wanted to provide a free Christmas dinner to the poor in San Francisco. He used a large crab pot to collect donations, inspiring the tradition.

- **Celebrity Bell Ringers**: Over the years, numerous celebrities, including former U.S. Presidents and Hollywood stars, have volunteered as bell ringers during the holiday season.
- **Annual Impact**: The Salvation Army assists approximately 23 million Americans annually, providing basic needs, rehabilitation services, and spiritual guidance.

Despite these controversies, The Salvation Army continues to be a major force in providing social services and disaster relief worldwide. Their ability to mobilize volunteers and resources quickly in times of need remains one of their strongest assets, though continuous efforts to improve transparency and accountability are essential. After all, even bell ringers need to know where the money's going.

#6. Feed the Children

Feed the Children is dedicated to alleviating childhood hunger and providing disaster relief. Despite its noble mission, the organization has been plagued by internal strife and accusations of financial mismanagement. Reports of in-fighting among the leadership and board members have diverted focus from its core mission.

Positive Impact

Feed the Children has managed to provide millions of meals and support to children in need. Their programs focus on both immediate hunger relief and long-term solutions, such as educational support and sustainable farming initiatives. The organization operates in many countries and helps vulnerable children and their families. In many communities, they are a beacon of hope, providing essentials that children might otherwise go without.

Criticisms and Challenges

- **Internal Strife**: The organization has faced significant internal challenges, including conflicts among its leadership and board members. These issues have led to instability and distracted from the core mission of feeding children. Reports of power struggles and mismanagement have eroded trust among donors and stakeholders.

It's hard to feed the children when you're busy with a food fight in the boardroom.

- **Financial Mismanagement**: Feed the Children has also been criticized for inefficient use of donations, with a significant portion of funds allegedly not reaching the intended beneficiaries. This has led to decreased donor trust and challenges in fulfilling its mission effectively. Transparency and accountability remain ongoing concerns for the organization. After all, if your donation is meant to provide meals, it shouldn't end up as another line item in a convoluted expense report.

Despite these issues, Feed the Children has still managed to provide critical support to millions of children and families. However, the organization's internal challenges highlight the importance of strong governance and transparent operations in maintaining donor confidence and achieving its mission. It's a reminder that even with the best intentions, organizational dysfunction can undermine charitable efforts.

#5. United Way

United Way is one of the largest and most recognized charities globally, focusing on community-based support and development. However, various scandals over the years, including cases of financial mismanagement and excessive executive compensation, have tarnished its reputation. And now, dear reader, we're halfway through our countdown to the most controversial charity revelations. The stakes are getting higher, so let's dive into the complexities of United Way.

Positive Impact

United Way has made significant contributions to communities worldwide, supporting education, financial stability, and health initiatives. The organization's widespread network and ability to mobilize local resources remain key strengths. United Way partners with local organizations to address community-specific needs, making a tangible impact on millions of lives. Their extensive reach allows them to touch diverse areas of need, from early childhood education to emergency disaster response.

Criticisms and Challenges

- **Financial Mismanagement**: The organization has faced multiple scandals involving financial mismanagement and embezzlement by top executives. One of the most notorious cases was that of William Aramony, the former CEO, who was convicted in 1995 for defrauding the United Way of America of $1.2 million. Aramony's lavish spending included using charity funds for personal luxuries and inappropriate activities, which severely damaged the organization's reputation.
- **Excessive Executive Compensation**: United Way has also been criticized for the high salaries and benefits of its top executives. In 2008, Gloria Pace King, CEO of United Way of Central Carolinas, received $1.2 million in compensation, sparking outrage among donors and the public. The excessive pay packages have raised questions about the organization's priorities and the effectiveness of its financial oversight.
- **Fund Allocation and Transparency**: United Way has faced scrutiny over its allocation of funds. Critics argue that a significant portion of donations is spent on administrative and fundraising costs rather than directly supporting community programs. For instance, donations directed to specific organizations through United Way are subject to a 10% fee, which includes administration and fundraising costs, potentially limiting the impact of donor contributions.

Despite these controversies, United Way continues to play a vital role in community development and support. Continuous efforts to improve transparency and accountability are essential to rebuilding trust and ensuring that donations are used effectively to achieve the organization's mission. They've made strides in addressing past issues, but the journey to full redemption is still a work in progress. Stay tuned as we inch closer to the top, revealing more jaw-dropping charity truths.

#4. The American Red Cross

The American Red Cross is undoubtedly a force for good, providing critical services in the aftermath of disasters and emergencies. Here are some highlights of their impactful work:

Positive Impact

- **Disaster Relief**: The Red Cross responds to more than 60,000 disasters every year, including hurricanes, wildfires, and home fires. They provide shelter, food, and emotional support to those affected.
- **Blood Services**: They supply about 40% of the nation's blood, collecting approximately 6.5 million blood donations annually from nearly 4.5 million donors. That's a lot of life-saving juice!
- **Health and Safety Training**: Millions of people receive Red Cross training in CPR, first aid, and water safety each year, equipping them with the skills to save lives.
- **Service to the Armed Forces**: The Red Cross provides support to military members, veterans, and their families, offering emergency communication services, financial assistance, and mental health resources.

Criticisms and Challenges

- **Financial Mismanagement**: In the wake of Hurricane Katrina, the Red Cross raised $2.1 billion for relief efforts. However, a significant portion of these funds was found to be mismanaged, with reports of money being used for administrative costs and other non-relief related expenses.
- **Questionable Spending**: Investigations have revealed that a considerable amount of donations are allocated to overhead and fundraising rather than direct services. For instance, during the 2010 Haiti earthquake relief effort, the Red Cross raised $500 million, but only a fraction of that went to direct aid, with much of it spent on internal expenses and partnerships that didn't yield significant results.
- **Blood Services Controversies**: The organization has faced numerous lawsuits and fines over the years related to blood safety. In 2012, they were fined $9.6 million by the FDA for mishandling blood products and failing to adhere to safety protocols.

CHARITY GIVING DONATION REVELATION

Quirky Facts and Trivia

- **Celebrity Blood Donors**: Did you know that celebrities like Nick Jonas and Taylor Swift have donated blood through Red Cross drives? Maybe they sang a little tune while donating.
- **Strange Donations**: Over the years, the Red Cross has received some bizarre donations, including a fully operational hovercraft and a pair of albino peacocks. It seems people sometimes confuse the Red Cross with Ripley's Believe It or Not!
- **Historic Missteps**: During the 1918 Spanish Flu pandemic, the Red Cross ran out of gauze masks and resorted to using fabric from petticoats. Talk about a wardrobe malfunction!

Financial Transparency Transparency is crucial for maintaining donor trust, and the Red Cross has made strides in this area, though not without hiccups.

- **Revenue**: In 2021, the Red Cross reported revenue of about $2.8 billion, sourced from donations, grants, and blood product sales.
- **Expense Allocation**: Approximately 91% of funds are directed towards program services, which include disaster relief, blood services, and health and safety training. The remaining 9% covers administrative and fundraising costs. However, critics argue that more should go directly to those in need.
- **Donor Concerns**: Transparency reports and independent audits are available, but some donors still feel there's a lack of detailed breakdowns on how their money is spent. This has led to calls for greater accountability and clearer reporting.

The American Red Cross is a venerable institution with a long history of providing crucial aid and services. However, like any large organization, it has its flaws and has faced significant criticisms. When we understand both the successes and the controversies, we can better see how complex its operations are and why ongoing scrutiny and improvement are important. So next time you see a Red Cross volunteer, give them a nod of respect—they're doing good work, even if the organization they represent sometimes stumbles along the way.

#3. Wounded Warrior Project

Wounded Warrior Project has undeniably done good work providing support, rehabilitation, and advocacy for wounded veterans. They offer programs to assist veterans in transitioning to civilian life, such as mental health support, career guidance, and adaptive sports. But as with many large organizations, not everything is as noble as it appears.

The Scandals and Missteps

- **Lavish Spending and Misuse of Funds**: In 2016, an explosive investigation by CBS News revealed that the Wounded Warrior Project was spending an exorbitant amount of donor money on lavish parties, luxury travel, and high salaries. Reports indicated that as much as 40-50% of donations were being used for overhead, including extravagant conferences at five-star resorts. The investigation showed that in one year, WWP spent around $26 million on conferences alone, leading many to question the organization's commitment to its mission versus its desire for a luxurious lifestyle.

- **Administrative Overhead**: A closer look at WWP's financial statements showed a significant portion of donations going towards administrative costs rather than veteran services. While WWP reported that 80% of their funds went to programs, critics argued that the actual amount spent directly on veterans was much lower when considering the inflated salaries and administrative expenses.

- **Leadership Shake-Up**: Following the damning reports, WWP faced a major leadership crisis. The CEO and COO were both fired, and the organization pledged to overhaul its operations and spending practices. This shake-up was meant to restore donor trust, but it also highlighted deep-seated issues within the charity's management.

- **Legal Battles and Donor Trust Issues**: The negative publicity led to a series of legal battles, including donor lawsuits alleging misrepresentation and fraud. These lawsuits further damaged WWP's reputation and led to a significant drop in donations as public trust waned.

Quirky Facts and Trivia

- **High Profile Supporters**: Despite the controversies, WWP has continued to enjoy support from high-profile celebrities and public figures, including actors like Mark Wahlberg and athletes like Kevin Durant.
- **Aggressive Fundraising**: WWP's aggressive fundraising tactics, including frequent mailings and telemarketing, have also drawn criticism for being overly intrusive and exploitative of donors' goodwill.
- **Programs Restructured**: In response to the scandals, WWP restructured many of its programs to ensure more funds were directly benefiting veterans, including the launch of new initiatives focused on mental health and peer support.

Financial Transparency

In the aftermath of the scandal, WWP made efforts to improve transparency and financial accountability:

- **Increased Program Spending**: Post-scandal, WWP claimed to increase the percentage of funds going directly to veteran programs. They now report that about 72% of donations are spent on programs, though scrutiny remains high.
- **Public Financial Statements**: WWP has made its financial statements more accessible and detailed, aiming to provide a clearer picture of how funds are allocated.

The Wounded Warrior Project's story is a cautionary tale about the perils of rapid growth and poor oversight in the nonprofit sector. Although they help veterans, their past mistakes remind us of the importance of being accountable and transparent. When donating to charities, remember that even good organizations can make mistakes, so it's important for donors to stay vigilant.

#2. Cancer Fund of America

The Cancer Fund of America (CFA) is a name that evokes trust and compassion. You'd expect that every penny donated would go towards fighting cancer and supporting patients. Unfortunately, what lies beneath is a staggering tale of deceit and mismanagement. So get ready as we unravel one of the most egregious charity scams of our time.

The Illusion of Good Intentions

On the surface, Cancer Fund of America seemed like a noble cause. Founded in 1987 by James T. Reynolds Sr., the charity purported to provide direct aid to cancer patients and fund cancer research. Donors were touched by the struggles of cancer patients and generously donated, hoping to make a big difference. In reality, the only significant impact was on the wallets of the organization's executives.

The Scandals and Missteps

- **Financial Mismanagement and Fraud**: The Cancer Fund of America, along with its affiliated charities (Breast Cancer Society, Children's Cancer Fund of America, and Cancer Support Services), was exposed in 2015 for gross financial mismanagement and fraudulent activities. A joint investigation by the Federal Trade Commission (FTC) and all 50 states revealed that less than 3% of the $187 million raised over eight years went to cancer patients. Instead, the money funded lavish lifestyles for the charity's operators, including luxury vacations, high salaries, and even dating site memberships.

- **Exorbitant Salaries and Perks**: James T. Reynolds Sr., the founder, and his family members received exorbitant salaries and perks. Reynolds Sr. paid himself over $1 million in salary, while family members were similarly compensated. The funds were also used for personal expenses, including cars, gym memberships, and cruises. It turns out charity does begin at home—specifically the Reynolds home.

- **Deceptive Fundraising Practices**: The charity employed aggressive and deceptive fundraising tactics, misleading donors about where their money was going. Telemarketers were instructed to tell potential donors that their contributions would go directly to cancer patients and research. In reality, most of the funds went to fundraising costs and administrative expenses, leaving a pittance for actual cancer-related activities.
- **Legal Action and Shut Down**: In 2015, the FTC along with 50 state attorneys general brought a lawsuit against the Cancer Fund of America and its affiliates. The lawsuit resulted in the shutdown of the organizations and a $75.8 million settlement. James T. Reynolds Sr. was banned from profiting from any charity fundraising ever again. A fitting end for an organization that misled and betrayed its donors so profoundly.

Quirky Facts and Trivia

- **Family Affair**: The Cancer Fund of America was essentially a family business, with multiple Reynolds family members holding high-paying positions within the charity.
- **Luxury Overload**: Instead of funding cancer research, donations paid for everything from jet skis to concert tickets. It seems they took the "fun" in fundraising a bit too literally.
- **Telemarketing Troubles**: The charity spent a staggering amount on telemarketing, with reports suggesting up to 85% of funds raised were funneled back into more fundraising rather than helping cancer patients.

Financial Transparency (or Lack Thereof)

Transparency was never a strong suit for the Cancer Fund of America. Their financial reports were murky at best, deliberately obfuscating how funds were spent. When scrutinized, it became clear that the vast majority of donations were used to sustain the fundraising machine and the lavish lifestyles of its operators.

- **Fundraising Costs**: Approximately 85% of the funds went towards paying professional telemarketers.
- **Administrative Costs**: Significant funds were diverted to cover the inflated salaries and personal expenses of the Reynolds family.
- **Direct Aid**: Less than 3% of the funds raised actually went to cancer patients or research.

The Cancer Fund of America stands as a stark reminder of the importance of due diligence when choosing where to donate your money. This organization preyed on the goodwill of donors, diverting millions away from those who needed it most. As we near the top of our list, remember that not all that glitters is gold and sometimes the seemingly most trustworthy charities can harbor the darkest secrets.

#1. Kids Wish Network

We've reached the pinnacle, the top of the heap, the absolute worst of the worst. Taking the gold medal in our list of scandalous charities is none other than the Kids Wish Network. This organization mishandled funds and deceived people while trying to grant wishes to sick children. So grab some popcorn and prepare to be appalled as we dive into the dark underbelly of Kids Wish Network.

The Illusion of Generosity

Kids Wish Network is a charity that grants wishes to children with life-threatening conditions, bringing them joy. From trips to Disney World to meeting celebrities, the narrative is designed to tug at your heartstrings and loosen your purse strings. Unfortunately, the reality is a far cry from the noble image they project.

The Scandals and Missteps

- **Astounding Mismanagement of Funds**: Investigations revealed that Kids Wish Network has consistently allocated less than 3% of donations to actually fulfilling wishes. Instead, a staggering 90% of the funds raised went to professional fundraisers and the organization's executives. Between 2008 and 2012, the charity raised nearly $128 million, but only $3.2 million went towards granting wishes. The rest lined the pockets of fundraisers and executives, making Kids Wish Network one of the most egregious examples of charity fraud.

- **Lavish Executive Compensation**: The charity's executives lived large on donor funds. The founder and CEO, Mark Breiner, and his family members received exorbitant salaries and benefits. In 2010, Breiner's compensation alone was reported to be over $250,000, a gross misuse of funds that should have gone to helping children. Meanwhile, millions of dollars were spent on luxury expenses rather than on the organization's stated mission.
- **Deceptive Fundraising Practices**: Kids Wish Network's fundraising tactics were aggressively misleading. They hired telemarketers who used emotional tactics to ask for donations, sometimes by saying the money would directly help sick children. In reality, the bulk of these donations went back into more fundraising efforts and administrative costs. This vicious cycle of deception ensured that very little money ever reached the intended beneficiaries.
- **Legal Scrutiny and Settlements**: The charity faced multiple legal challenges and settlements due to its fraudulent activities. Kids Wish Network was fined $110,000 by California in 2014 for deceptive practices, but they actually misused hundreds of millions over the years. Even with fines and more attention, the organization still operated, making people trust charitable giving even less.

Quirky Facts and Trivia

- **Worst Charity Award**: Kids Wish Network has frequently topped the lists of worst charities in America, earning the dubious distinction of being the most wasteful and least effective in terms of donor dollars reaching their intended cause.
- **Family Affair**: The charity operated much like a family business, with key positions filled by relatives and close associates of the founder, ensuring that the wealth stayed within a small, tight-knit circle.
- **Non-Wish Spending**: Astonishingly, the organization spent more on

office supplies and staff salaries than on actually fulfilling wishes, highlighting their skewed priorities.

Financial Transparency (or Lack Thereof)
Kids Wish Network's financial practices were shrouded in opacity.

- **Revenue**: Raised nearly $128 million from 2008 to 2012, largely through telemarketing and direct mail campaigns.
- **Fundraising Costs**: Approximately 90% of the raised funds went to professional fundraisers.
- **Direct Aid**: Less than 3% of the donations were used to fulfill the wishes of sick children, the very mission they claimed to support.

Kids Wish Network is a charity that mismanages funds and uses the goal of helping children as a way to make money for its leaders and fundraisers. This charity stands as a stark reminder of the importance of due diligence and transparency in the nonprofit sector. As you consider your next charitable donation, remember the cautionary tale of Kids Wish Network and choose wisely. It's a wild world out there in charity land, and not all that glitters is gold.

Great Big Grab Bag of Useless Trivia

1. **The Most Unusual Items Ever Donated: Wedding Dresses**
    Organizations like Brides Across America collect wedding dresses
    and give them to military brides in need. This initiative helps military
    families afford beautiful weddings and runs several donation events
    throughout the year across the U.S.

2. **Records for the Largest Single Donations: Bill Gates and Melinda
    French Gates**
    Their 2010 donation of $10 billion to the Bill & Melinda Gates
    Foundation supports global health initiatives, including the fight
    against infectious diseases and improving education worldwide.

3. **Quirky Charity Events and Fundraisers: Goat Yoga**
    This unique fundraising event combines yoga sessions with playful
    goats. Proceeds support local animal shelters and farms. Events are
    held periodically in various locations and can be found through local
    event listings or yoga studios.

4. **Longest Charity Run: Rob Young**
    Set the record for the longest charity run by covering 10,000 miles
    across the UK in 420 days, raising funds for various children's
    charities. This feat took place from 2014 to 2015, and his journey can
    be followed through his book and social media accounts.

5. **Floating Libraries: Pakistan Flood Relief**
    In 2010, volunteers set up "floating libraries" on boats to provide
    books and educational materials to children stranded by floodwaters.
    This innovative approach supported continuous learning despite the
    disaster's disruption.

6. **Anonymous Giver: Chuck Feeney**
    Co-founder of Duty-Free Shoppers, quietly gave away his entire $8
    billion fortune, earning him the nickname "The James Bond of
    Philanthropy." His story is detailed in the book "The Billionaire Who
    Wasn't" by Conor O'Clery.

7. **Power of the Beard: Richard Branson**
    Shaved his iconic beard after raising over $1 million for a children's

charity in 2009. This quirky fundraising stunt was part of Virgin's extensive charitable activities.

8. **Largest Food Drive: Scouting for Food**
An annual event organized by the Boy Scouts of America, collecting millions of pounds of food for local food banks. This drive occurs every November across the U.S., with local Scout troops participating.

9. **Most Generous Animal: Dogs in the U.K.**
Known for participating in charity events like sponsored walks and even skydives to raise funds for animal shelters. Events are often organized by local animal welfare groups and can be found through their websites.

10. **Unusual Charity Auction Items: Lunch with Warren Buffett**
An annual charity auction where bidders can win a lunch with Warren Buffett, raising millions for the Glide Foundation. The auction is held every year on eBay.

11. **Celebrity Charity Boxing Matches: Fight for Kids**
Celebrities participate in boxing matches to raise money for children's charities. These events are often televised and organized by major charity organizations, featuring celebrities from various industries.

12. **Longest Charity Dance Marathon: Penn State's THON**
The largest student-run philanthropy in the world, Penn State's THON is an annual 46-hour dance marathon to raise funds for pediatric cancer. Started in 1973, it involves thousands of students and raises millions of dollars each year.

13. **The Big Bake**
An annual event where participants bake and sell goods to support various causes. Typically held in community centers and schools across the U.S. during the fall, the Big Bake raises funds for local charities and community projects.

14. **High-Tech Charity: Foldit**
An online puzzle game where players help scientists with protein folding, contributing to biomedical research. Launched in 2008, Foldit can be accessed from anywhere with an internet connection,

allowing participants worldwide to contribute to scientific discoveries.

15. **Most Miles Walked for Charity: The Walk of Hope**
A 4,000-mile walk across the U.S. to raise awareness and funds for cancer research. Initially undertaken as a one-time event, it inspired annual walks and smaller regional events. More information can be found on the event's website.

16. **Shoes for All: Soles4Souls**
A global nonprofit that collects and distributes new and gently worn shoes to people in need. Since its inception in 2006, Soles4Souls has distributed over 30 million pairs of shoes in 127 countries. Donation drives are held throughout the year in various locations.

17. **Coins for Change: Club Penguin**
A virtual world event where players donate virtual coins to real-world causes. Held annually during the holiday season from 2007 until 2017, Coins for Change allowed players to choose which global projects to support, demonstrating the power of virtual philanthropy.

18. **Hair Today, Gone Tomorrow: Locks of Love**
A nonprofit that provides hairpieces to financially disadvantaged children suffering from long-term medical hair loss. Founded in 1997, Locks of Love accepts hair donations from individuals across the U.S. and hosts cutting events at salons nationwide.

19. **World's Largest Garage Sale: The 127 Corridor Sale**
Spanning 690 miles from Michigan to Alabama, this massive annual garage sale supports local charities and small businesses. Held the first Thursday through Sunday in August, it attracts thousands of shoppers and sellers each year.

20. **Art for Charity: The Sketchbook Project**
A global, crowd-sourced art project and interactive library that allows anyone to submit a sketchbook to be included in a permanent collection. Based in Brooklyn, NY, it has grown since its start in 2006, supporting various art-related charities and community projects.

21. **Pajama Program**
Provides new pajamas and books to children in need, particularly

those in foster care and homeless shelters. Since its founding in 2001, the Pajama Program has distributed millions of pajamas and books across the U.S. through donation drives and events.

22. **Cycling for Water: WaterAid's Cycle Challenge**
An annual cycling event where participants ride across countries to raise funds and awareness for clean water projects. Events have taken place in various countries, including the UK, Australia, and Canada. Riders can join pre-organized events or create their own routes.

23. **Climb for Charity: Climb for Clean Air**
A mountaineering program that raises funds for the American Lung Association. Participants climb iconic peaks like Mt. Rainier and Mt. Hood, receiving training and support for their fundraising efforts. The climbs occur annually, typically during the summer months.

24. **Run Across America: The Relay**
A 200-mile team relay race that raises funds for various charities, including cancer research and disaster relief. Teams of runners take turns running segments of the course, which spans from Southern California to San Francisco. The event is held annually in the spring.

25. **Charity Pub Quizzes**
Local bars and pubs host quiz nights to raise money for various causes. These events combine entertainment with philanthropy, drawing in participants with the promise of fun and the opportunity to support charities. They are often held weekly or monthly in cities worldwide.

26. **Book Donation Drives: Room to Read**
Collects books and funds to support literacy and education programs in developing countries. Founded in 2000, Room to Read organizes book drives and fundraising events globally, helping millions of children gain access to education.

27. **Marathons for a Cause: Team in Training**
The Leukemia & Lymphoma Society's flagship fundraising program, where participants train for marathons, triathlons, and cycling events while raising money for blood cancer research. Founded in 1988, Team in Training has raised over $1.5 billion.

28. **Plant a Tree: Arbor Day Foundation**

Hosts tree-planting events and campaigns to support reforestation and environmental conservation. Founded in 1972, the Arbor Day Foundation encourages individuals and communities to plant trees, offering resources and organizing large-scale planting events.

29. **Comedy for a Cause: Comic Relief**
A UK-based charity that uses comedy to raise funds for various causes, including poverty and social injustice. Founded in 1985, Comic Relief hosts events like Red Nose Day, featuring comedians and celebrities, raising millions each year.

30. **Volunteer Vacations: Habitat for Humanity's Global Village**
Allows volunteers to travel and help build homes for those in need worldwide. Since 1989, the Global Village program has sent volunteers to over 70 countries, combining travel with meaningful service work.

31. **Gifts That Give Back: Heifer International**
Provides livestock and agricultural training to help communities become self-sufficient. Founded in 1944, Heifer International allows donors to give gifts like cows, goats, and chickens to families in need, supporting sustainable development.

32. **Soup Kitchen Fundraisers: Empty Bowls**
An international project to fight hunger, where participants create and sell handmade bowls, with proceeds going to local food banks and soup kitchens. The events are held in communities worldwide, typically in the fall and winter months.

33. **The Great Knitathon: Warm Up America!**
Volunteers knit and crochet blankets, clothing, and accessories for people in need. Founded in 1991, Warm Up America! organizes knitting events and drives throughout the year, encouraging crafters to donate their handmade items.

34. **Caroling for Charity: Christmas Carols**
Groups sing holiday carols door-to-door to raise money for various causes. This tradition dates back centuries and continues to be a popular way to spread holiday cheer and support charities during the festive season.

35. **Dancing for a Cure: Dance Marathon**

College and high school students participate in dance marathons to raise money for children's hospitals and medical research. These events, often lasting 12-24 hours, are held annually at schools across the U.S., raising millions for pediatric care.

36. **Charity Concerts: Live Aid**

One of the most famous charity concerts, held in 1985 to raise funds for famine relief in Ethiopia. Organized by Bob Geldof and Midge Ure, Live Aid featured performances by major artists and raised over $125 million.

37. **Easter Egg Hunts: Charity Hunts**

Communities organize Easter egg hunts to raise funds for local charities. These events typically involve a small entry fee, with proceeds going to support various causes. They are held annually around Easter in parks and community centers.

38. **Charity Golf Tournaments: Drive for Life**

Golf enthusiasts participate in tournaments to raise money for cancer research and other causes. These events are often sponsored by corporations and held at prestigious golf courses, combining sport with philanthropy.

39. **Polar Bear Plunges: Freezin' for a Reason**

Brave souls plunge into icy waters to raise funds for various charities. Polar Bear Plunges are held annually in winter months, often on New Year's Day, with participants soliciting donations for their daring feat.

40. **Read-a-Thons: Book It Forward**

Participants read books to raise money for literacy programs and libraries. Read-a-thons encourage reading while supporting educational initiatives, often organized by schools and libraries.

41. **Walkathons: Making Strides Against Breast Cancer**

An annual series of walking events organized by the American Cancer Society to raise funds and awareness for breast cancer research. Held in cities across the U.S., these walks draw millions of participants each year.

42. **Charity Auctions: Bid for Good**

Online and live auctions where items and experiences are auctioned off to raise money for various causes. These events are often organized by nonprofits and feature unique and high-value items.

43. **Bake Sales: Cookies for Kids' Cancer**

A nonprofit that raises funds for pediatric cancer research through bake sales. Founded in 2008, Cookies for Kids' Cancer encourages communities to host bake sales and donate proceeds to support cancer research.

44. **Fun Runs: Color Run**

Participants run through courses while being doused in colored powder, raising money for various charities. The Color Run, known as the "Happiest 5K on the Planet," is held annually in cities worldwide.

45. **Charity Galas: Black Tie for a Cause**

Formal events where attendees dress in black tie attire and participate in auctions, raffles, and other activities to raise funds for charities. These glamorous events are often held at luxury venues and attract high-profile guests.

46. **Pet Adoption Events: Rescue Me**

Animal shelters and rescue organizations host adoption events to find homes for pets and raise funds for their care. These events are held throughout the year, often in collaboration with pet stores and community centers.

47. **Charity Fashion Shows: Catwalk for a Cause**

Fashion shows where designers and models showcase their work to raise money for various causes. These events often feature celebrity guests and are held in major fashion capitals like New York and Paris.

48. **Penny Drives: Change for Change**

Schools and communities collect pennies and other loose change to support local charities. Penny drives are simple yet effective fundraisers, often held during the school year.

49. **Charity Bingo Nights**

Local communities organize bingo nights to raise money for various causes. These events combine entertainment with philanthropy, drawing in participants with the promise of fun and prizes.

50. **Virtual Charity Challenges: Step Up for a Cause**

Participants use fitness trackers to log steps or miles for charity, raising funds based on their activity levels. These virtual challenges can be joined from anywhere, making them accessible and popular fundraisers.

Charity Evaluation Sites

1. **Charity Navigator**: www.charitynavigator.org[1]
   - Provides ratings based on financial health, accountability, and transparency of thousands of charities.
2. **GuideStar**: www.guidestar.org[2]
   - Offers comprehensive data on nonprofit organizations, including financial statements and impact reports.
3. **BBB Wise Giving Alliance**: www.give.org[3]
   - Evaluates charities based on 20 standards of accountability, including governance and effectiveness.
4. **GiveWell**: www.givewell.org[4]
   - Focuses on identifying the most effective charities through in-depth research and analysis.
5. **CharityWatch**: www.charitywatch.org[5]
   - Provides detailed ratings and analyses of nonprofit organizations based on rigorous standards.

---

1. https://www.charitynavigator.org

2. https://www.guidestar.org

3. https://www.give.org

4. https://www.givewell.org

5. https://www.charitywatch.org

Recommended Books and Articles

1. **"The Billionaire Who Wasn't" by Conor O'Clery**
   - A biography of Chuck Feeney, co-founder of Duty-Free Shoppers, who gave away his entire fortune anonymously.
2. **"Give and Take" by Adam Grant**
   - Explores the dynamics of giving and how generosity can lead to success in business and life.
3. **"Doing Good Better" by William MacAskill**
   - An introduction to effective altruism, offering practical advice on how to make the greatest impact with charitable donations.
4. **"Philanthropy Revolution" by Lisa Greer**
   - Provides insights from a major donor on how charities can build trust and transparency with donors.
5. **"Charity Case" by Dan Pallotta**
   - Argues for a new way of thinking about charity and nonprofit work to maximize impact.
6. **Articles from the Harvard Business Review:**
   - "The Hidden Costs of Cause Marketing" explores potential pitfalls of cause-marketing strategies.
   - "How Nonprofits Can Make the Most of Donor-Advised Funds" discusses strategies for leveraging this growing source of charitable giving.

Contact Information for Major Charities

1. **American Red Cross**
   - Website: www.redcross.org[1]
   - Phone: 1-800-RED-CROSS (1-800-733-2767)
2. **UNICEF**
   - Website: www.unicef.org[2]
   - Phone: 1-800-367-5437
3. **Doctors Without Borders (Médecins Sans Frontières)**
   - Website: www.doctorswithoutborders.org[3]
   - Phone: 1-888-392-0392
4. **Habitat for Humanity**
   - Website: www.habitat.org[4]
   - Phone: 1-800-HABITAT (1-800-422-4828)
5. **Feeding America**
   - Website: www.feedingamerica.org[5]
   - Phone: 1-800-771-2303
6. **St. Jude Children's Research Hospital**
   - Website: www.stjude.org[6]
   - Phone: 1-800-822-6344
7. **The Nature Conservancy**
   - Website: www.nature.org[7]
   - Phone: 1-800-628-6860
8. **World Wildlife Fund (WWF)**
   - Website: www.worldwildlife.org[8]

---

1. https://www.redcross.org

2. https://www.unicef.org

3. https://www.doctorswithoutborders.org

4. https://www.habitat.org

5. https://www.feedingamerica.org

6. https://www.stjude.org

7. https://www.nature.org

8. https://www.worldwildlife.org

- Phone: 1-800-960-0993
9. **American Cancer Society**
    - Website: www.cancer.org[9]
    - Phone: 1-800-227-2345
10. **The Salvation Army**
    - Website: www.salvationarmyusa.org[10]
    - Phone: 1-800-SAL-ARMY (1-800-725-2769)

---

9. https://www.cancer.org

10. https://www.salvationarmyusa.org

About the Author

Michael P. Clutton isn't your typical storyteller. Since he was young, he loved drawing cartoons and writing stories, which not only kept him busy but also helped him learn more words. This early passion for fiction laid the foundation for his unique voice—rich, imaginative, and brimming with wit.

Michael's sarcastic and unique perspective on life adds intrigue to his daily routine and captivates those around him. Known for his quick wit and self-deprecating humor, he can generate a giggle or a guffaw at the drop of a hat. His creative toolbox is well-stocked with both artwork and the written word, making him a versatile and dynamic creator.

Discover the captivating world of Michael P. Clutton, an author who combines humor, heart, and a deep passion for creativity in his stories and art.

Read more at www.michaelpclutton.com.